To Susan,
with much love
and gratitude,
Boston GA, 2003 *Judit*

Prisoner of Liberté

The Story of a Transylvanian Martyr

Judit Gellérd

Uniquest
Chico, CA

Copyright © by Judit Gellérd

Printed in the U.S.A

Uniquest
A division of New Horizons Press
P.O. Box 1758
Chico, CA. 95927

ISBN 0-914914-18-9

CONTENTS

PROLOGUE   1
     Vertical Time
CHAPTER 1   2
     The Shepherd
     The Power of Excellence
     The First Dilemma, Then the Rest
     The Years of Intellectual Thriving
     Dance Macabre
CHAPTER 2   12
     The War Loses its Sting
     The City Lost its Innocence
     "We Either Win Him Over or Destroy Him"
CHAPTER 3   18
     In Love
     Princess in Captivity—Judit's Saga
     Ambivalence of Destiny
     Sobbing Bride
     Sowing and Reaping
CHAPTER 4   34
     Idealism at Work
     Academia and Politics, Victories and Tribulations
CHAPTER 5   41
     The Black Jeep
     Secret Police Face to Face
     Where is My Father?
     The Grand Theater of an Evil Empire
CHAPTER 6   53
     The Art of Prison Living
     Subtle Tortures
     Time Measured in Christmases
     The Romanian Gulag
     Traps for Judit
     Coerced Suicide—a Clean Murder
CHAPTER 7   70
     The Failed Attempt
     Dying a Little at a Time

Re-education
The Crisis of Freedom
Where to Go?
Embroidered Rags
Unforgiveness
CHAPTER 8   81
Unwelcome
Healing Alone
Typically Bankrupt
The Bells of Time
CHAPTER 9   92
Crises and Opportunities
Irony in Grief
Underestimated Determination
Ray of Light
Daughter's Dilemma
Final Marginalization
A Mere Epilogue
CHAPTER 10   107
Parenting
Simple Serenity
Hostile Borders, Fake Marriage
The Departing Train
CHAPTER 11   115
New Threats
Wings With No Space to Fly
Christmas
No Good-Bye
Blood on Red Carnation
The Escape
CHAPTER 12   126
Over the Abyss
Thunder
Bound by Light
EPILOGUE   131

ACKNOWLEDGMENT

During my most recent graduate studies at Boston University School of Theology, I had the rare privilege of being a student of Nobel Peace laureate professor Elie Wiesel. He activated in me a sense of urgency to contribute to the literature of witness by writing about Communist totalitarianism based on my father's story. For his inspiration and guidance I am immensely indebted. I am also committed to continue this witness with the stories of my own life.

My gratitude is also due to the Unitarian Universalist Funding Program for their generosity in honoring my oral history project by partially funding this publication. I also thank those UU congregations and friends who, touched by my father's writings, encouraged me to write his life story and his search for meaning in the midst of dehumanization.

Since my father told me the story of his prison years only once, I needed to fill in some of the details of prison life. I interviewed some of his surviving prisonmates and consulted the book of Calvinist pastor Rev. László Varga. In gratitude, I dedicate this book to them and to the memory of those who senselessly suffered and died during the reign of Communist terror in my Transylvania homeland.

I am deeply thankful for my faithful editor Kenneth Mitchel, whose contributions should be appreciated by the reader. Always catching the intended meaning, he proved invaluable. His insights testify to his sensitivity for the spirit of the book.

I further wish to express my gratitude to my brother Andor Gellérd and my life-long friends Gabriella Koszta, Dénes Farkas and Matild Szabó-Crawford as well as my English teacher, Lilly Sibelka-Perleberg, for their encouragement and advice. Thanks are also due to my shipmates and my students on the *Semester at Sea* program.

My mother Judit Kovács's own memoir, written at my request, is a priceless gift to her children and serves as a crucial document and source of inspiration for which I am deeply grateful.

Finally, my husband George M. Williams, is more than a source of inspiration and a patient listener of my stories, he is a blessing for us Transylvanians, now as in the past.

Judit (Zizi) Gellérd
May 2003

1

PROLOGUE

Vertical Time

T omorrow he would have been sixty. But there was no tomorrow. My father hovered above the abyss between life and death. His life reverberated in a cacophony, while the eternal stillness lured him irrevocably. Time was vertical for him now. It was that time when God's impenetrable language of life decoded itself. He was too obstinate in trying to interpret that language as *happiness*. He had given God enough chances, but the blind wandering of the covenant seemed to lead nowhere. Why should he march, once again, into the prison of the *Securitate*? The Securitate [Romania's Secret Police] would arrest him soon. He had lived in consuming fear. He had wasted hope too long. He could endure torture no more.

He had preached his last sermon today, imploring his congregation: "God does not expect you to save the world. Your mandate is limited to one single human being, which may be just yourself—or your neighbor. God never expects more from us than we are capable of doing. Each word of comfort, each act of compassion, is a small bonfire in the thundering nights. But these tiny flickering flames, the simple gestures of loving hearts, will add up and will eventually save the world. Salvation is not something we have to wait for, but we must do something about. Because we can. Because we can, therefore we must."

Therefore we must! The words echoed in his mind. He had crawled too long in cages. There had been too few words of comfort in the endless darkness. He had to free himself at last. He had to seek another path to salvation, even if that were a fatal shortcut. It became his mandate to glimpse his life from the *other* side, for he wanted to believe that his life ultimately had meaning. His faith was at stake, and he offered his life in exchange.

CHAPTER 1

The Shepherd

Green meadows and fleecy clouds surrounded him. A little shepherd pastured his Easter lambs. He was small, too small for his age. His bare foot was bleeding—but of course, he was from Kénos, the smallest village of Transylvania, and Kénos meant "painful" in Hungarian. He was earning his shoes, actually. The pride of this orphan boy was unusual. An inner fire transcended his malnourished body. He held his head high, as if gazing into some impending splendor. It was stirring to look into his eyes. But he was a nobody!

He was Imre Gellérd, a ten-year-old.

* * *

The memories of that summer broke into Imre's fading consciousness. He had almost forgotten the brightness of those summers when he was still with his parents. Happiness then was simple and abundant—the smell of freshly ploughed fields, the bittersweet aroma of parching hay, the closeness of the earth. The fields were still around him but had lost their color and fragrance. All that he was left with was longing. The longing consumed him.

* * *

With the birds as their waking alarm, the sunrise found the Gellérd family out in the fields of their farm. The physically smallest among the four children, Imre worked as hard as anyone. He had developed a technique of dividing his attention between the hoe and a book that he carried everywhere. He transposed the reading of the written lines into the hoeing of the rows. He always took the lane next to his father, where he could smell his father's heavy perspiration. Ferenc was a real man. A veteran of World War I, he was full of fascinating stories of battles and captivities, of forced marches on endless snow fields, and of strangers' mercy in the gift of a piece of bread that saved his life. Neighbors gathered in his kitchen to listen to Ferenc Gellérd's saga. Imre loved being a child of his father.

The state of blessedness suddenly ended when the black cloud of death took his father. People say that disasters come in clusters, and this was true in their home. His mother, a simple peasant woman, soon became

3

entrapped in a lawsuit. She was defenseless against the various legal manipulations of the time and in due course the family estate was lost. Imre had been confronted with human greed and cruelty for the first time. Before his eleventh birthday he had become fatherless and destitute almost overnight. The five of them huddled together which gave him some comfort, but not for long. With an ill-conceived compassion, their relatives in Kénos offered a safer haven for at least one child. Without much consultation with their mother, they chose Imre and ripped him from his mother's arms. The place where he was taken was actually not far from the parental home, and he could have visited if he had had the freedom and shoes to walk over a few hills. Perhaps he was expected to be grateful, but it never occurred to him at that time. He was supposed to go back to school. Instead, the status of the village shepherd was ceremonially bestowed upon him. Having no choice, he decided to make the best of it and become a good shepherd. A shepherd with dignity.

As long as the summer and his hopes lasted, his principal misery, aside from his loneliness, was his infected, bleeding feet. Yet more than the physical pain, his real suffering came from being deprived from learning. His foster parents, as they called themselves, ruthlessly confiscated his books upon his arrival. "You are just a peasant, orphaned and penniless! What on earth do you want?" They wanted to cut his wings and choke his dreams which were deemed useless for a shepherd. Taking away his books, however, did not prevent him from reading. Now he read the stories that he wrote in his mind.

His craving for knowledge finally forced him to break rules. One day he stole his books back, along with some candles. He slept in the barn— the shepherds' bedroom—which in the candlelight suddenly became a luxurious place of stolen freedom. Those were good days.

Then with the cold and rainy autumn, his anxiety turned into agony as his hopes for a miraculous intervention dwindled. His wages eventually provided enough for a pair of boots, the sole condition for school attendance, he thought. By mid-October, however, he had to realize that he was stranded in this beyond-the-reach-of-God place where no one would come to rescue him and take him to school.

It was the village's Unitarian minister who finally brought him liberation. With a strange solemnity in his voice, the minister informed the foster parents that the boy was too gifted to waste his life there. It was a conversation Imre would never forget. He was soon sent back to his mother—with his new pair of boots.

While his father was alive they had lived in a large home on the outskirts of Székelyudvarhely [Odorheiul Secuiesc].[1] Now the family crowded into a small cottage. Yet even poverty tasted sweet at home. Their mother's simple purity and the warmth of her love nurtured an intense sense of happiness in Imre. What he could not bear was her daily drudgery, as she tried to earn a meager living as a washer woman. Her son's shepherd instinct urged him to be her protector, whatever that might mean.

The Power of Excellence

Imre re-entered school and was eventually accepted at the prestigious "Stefan Octavian" high school. Although this was a most awaited moment, this school was not his choice. It was a Romanian school, and Imre was Hungarian. Nobody held his hand when he first entered this foreign place, where he did not understand a word, yet where he would spend the next eight years.

Imre's high school education brought into focus an historical schism in Eastern Europe that began in 1920, the year of his birth. Under the Treaty of Trianon, much of Transylvania became part of Romania. Imre's ancestors were all Hungarian, but his mother's citizenship changed to Romanian overnight. Imre had no experience of the "good old times" his parents' generation lamented about. While they grumbled about compulsory oath of allegiance to the Romanian state which they were required to sign as a condition to keep their state jobs, Imre became fluent in Romanian and embraced the foreign language education as the only available. He did not understand until later that taking the oath compromised Hungarians' integrity and national dignity. Only much later did he see that no one should have to face the humiliating choice of maintaining family security or upholding national identity. Hungarians seemed to be losers either way and were torn by conflicting loyalties. Many of those who were faithful to their moral principles, left their homeland and livelihood to immigrate to Hungary or America.

Imre was too young to sense the moral dimension in his ambition to conform to the situation he was born into. His will to succeed and help his mother dominated his inner world. For this reason there was something exhilarating for this poor, small teenage boy to experience increasingly the respect of the all-powerful Romanian teachers and well-to-do

---

[1]The name in brackets is the current Romanian place name.

classmates. He was never beaten up in school. He hardly ever went home hungry; his classmates shared their lunches with him. This was triumph.

One beautiful autumn day an elegant carriage stopped in front of their cottage, like in the fairy tales. It was the Romanian mayor's "chariot," sent for Imre. The mayor's son was his classmate, and Imre had visited their house before, helping his classmate with his homework—and being rewarded with cocoa and sweet bread by the boy's mother. This time the father himself greeted him and offered him a real job, to be his son's paid tutor. Each afternoon thereafter the luxury coach carried him to the mayor's palace!

Soon more middle class families, Hungarian and Romanian, invited Imre to tutor their children. So, for the next seven years, he ate several dinners every night and earned a decent living for the family. The joy of teaching was intoxicating, and the child in him loved the sweet treats. The best part was their neighbors' amazement and respect for the high status of the poor widow's son. Imre tasted the power of excellence and he never wanted to give it up.

At age thirteen Imre became the breadwinner for his mother, his two brothers and his sister. He earned enough money to free his mother from day labor. At that time she was pregnant and later gave birth to another boy.

Imre loved school. He loved his Romanian teachers. He was truly bilingual, and it never occurred to him that his ethnic rights were being violated. He hardly ever experienced discrimination in school. In fact, this essentially anti-minority school rewarded him with scholarships and the highest annual merit awards. Doors toward success seemed to open before him when he received his baccalaureate [B.A. degree] in 1939.

The First Dilemma, Then the Rest

Imre carried an uncomfortable secret throughout his childhood. On his birth certificate he was registered as a Roman Catholic. His mother would lightly dismiss his inquiries as a clerical mistake. Their family was obviously Unitarian and it always had been. The immediate community in which they lived, however, was almost entirely Roman Catholic, and he was probably automatically taken as such. One might think that after accommodating his education in his second language with such ease, religious affiliation carried a lesser weight. For the nineteen-year-old Imre, however, his Unitarian faith had become a sensitive issue. Few ever changed religions in Transylvania. There was no fluidity between denominations. People were born into *their* religion.

Imre took personal pride in the fact that *his* faith, Unitarianism, was the only religion indigenous to Transylvania and to Hungarian culture. The first Western proclamation and practice of religious tolerance was by his tradition! His essence was that very freedom of conscience that Unitarianism had set forth in the sixteenth century. Being a Unitarian for him meant a total commitment, a passionate, active existence. But some dissonance surfaced in this passion, an irrational attraction for the Catholic faith. The more this ambiguity became conscious, the more he tried to deny it and prove that his Unitarian commitment was clear-cut. He couldn't imagine a compromise in this matter. Or could he?

The decisive influence in his formative years came from the town's Unitarian minister József Sigmond. The parsonage of Székelyudvarhely became Imre's second home, his spiritual home. He found a much needed father in Rev. Sigmond. He supported him in every way. His enthusiastic and energetic nature destined him to a leadership role in the local youth organization. Rev. Sigmond did not make a secret of his desire to see Imre become a Unitarian minister. This was his mother's wish also. Both urged him to apply to the Theological Academy at Kolozsvár [Cluj].

Imre's ambivalent nature now posed a dilemma. As much as he desired to rise and break through his social limitations, now he was about to recoil from the opportunity. As with many poor children, he dreamed of becoming a teacher or a minister. Villages of Transylvania had been the sources of generations of intellectuals. He believed he was destined to carry on the tradition, he sensed the call. But his inherited instinct of a farmer was strong and binding. His attachment to the soil was luring him back, its voice was robust—a chorus of his ancestors. Now he was about to betray them. He felt a threat of losing his identity.

He ultimately had to realize that he no longer belonged to that rustic world. His wings were growing and the heights were itching them. He wanted to soar. He prayed, asking God to show him the right path. The realization came with revelatory power: instead of trying to choose between conflicting loyalties, he would combine the two calls into a harmonious unity. He would embrace the learning, and use it in the service of those faithful to the farmland. He would serve God's people in the villages of Transylvania. This reconciliatory solution filled him with peace.

The Years of Intellectual Thriving

In the fall of 1939 Imre left his hometown for the great city of Kolozsvár to enroll in the Unitarian Theological Academy. That was the right place for him. He loved nothing more than being in the pulpit. His words called forth a kingdom of justice and truth. He had words so powerful that they would change people's lives. His words would intimate the sublime presence of God. He would uphold the mighty fortress of divine love. His words would comfort and heal the broken-hearted. He would graft roses into children's souls.

The first challenge was the yearly preaching competition, a grand fun event in the life of the seminary. His main rival, the "other" Imre (Remetei Filep, a future bishop of Hungary,) was already a famous preacher, a senior. Imre Gellérd was just a freshman, but he won the contest. He won lots of attention too. From then on his sermons were among the prized ones of their weekly assignments. He also began to write poetry and compose music. He taught himself to play the piano and the organ. When he was a second-year student, he played organ recitals in the church. Life was intense; he was overflowing with joy, which made him sing, always sing!

His need for knowledge was as vital as his need for fresh air. Imre had the gift of a photographic memory. He couldn't help it; anything he had ever read, he remembered verbatim. He was plain lucky, and he took advantage of it. In the fall of 1941 he committed himself to additional university studies for the next five years. He enrolled at the prestigious University of Sciences at Kolozsvár (later Bolyai University) while he continued his seminary studies. He was blessed with the dilemma of plenitude. He thrived. His language studies of Latin, Hebrew and Greek at the seminary widened with five years of French and Romanian. He studied philosophy, psychology, pedagogy and sociology. Marxism at that time was a philosophers' delicacy. He first approached it as a forbidden fruit. but in his strong inclination toward socialist ideals, Imre found Marxist social analysis—and the parallels with gospel ideals—fascinating and honorable. By the time he graduated he was considered a Marxist expert, a rare scholarship for a Transylvanian at that time.

His true passion was child psychology and pedagogy. He was privileged to be invited by the renowned psychologist and author István Benedek to be his research assistant. He honored Imre with his attention and encouragement for a career in psychology. Together conducted fascinating child psychology studies. Imre knew then that he would become a lifelong student and teacher.

Dance Macabre

Europe's *dance macabre* of World War II grew into a dark background for Imre's blissful student life. The seminarians were shielded from the threat of being drafted, for they were exempted from serving in the military. The Unitarian Church discouraged its ministers and seminarians from active participation in political life too. Imre's close connection with the faculty and students of the university, however, drew him closer to the sources of alarming information from the fronts.

Strangely, none of them heard about the death marches and pogroms against the Romanian Jews by the Iron Guard, starting as early as 1938. This partly Gestapo-trained Romanian fascist organization had originally been an extreme right-wing student movement. Later it grew into the paramilitary anti-Semitic terror organization. They volunteered to exterminate Jews and Gypsies much earlier than Hitler's *Endlosung,* and outdid it with their horrific imagination for evil. Close to 400,000 Romanian Jews were slaughtered by the Iron Guard. In September of 1940, Ion Antonescu, Romania's wartime dictator, took power. Out of rivalry, he limited the power of the Iron Guard. The indigenous and voluntary Romanian Holocaust, however, was carefully kept secret and absolutely denied by the Romanian fascist government.

By the time Antonescu took power, Imre no longer was citizen of Romania. Not that he ever left his city—the borders moved over his head. In the summer of 1940, Imre suddenly became a Hungarian citizen. After twenty years of Romanian rule, Northern Transylvania was returned to Hungary once again. The world had hardly ever seen such public demonstrations of Hungarian national pride, as during the march of the victorious Hungarian army into Transylvania's cities. The Transylvanian Hungarian population lavishly exalted the troops. This was the first time in Imre's life that they openly sang'*their* national anthem, the ancient prayer *God Bless the Hungarians,* instead of the Romanian nationalist anthem *Long Live the King, Peace and Honor!*

Imre tasted the meaning of being at home in his ethnicity for the first time. He plunged more passionately than ever into turning his idealism into social actions. He was too busy to pay any more attention to the war. Or, perhaps denial was his self-defense. The war was too close and too threatening to dare to admit to the imminent danger they were in. In the midst of death around them, life exuberantly demanded its rights. He had never been more alive than in the shadow of cataclysm. No powers could deter him in his march toward realizing his dreams. He was elected student president of the Seminary. He regularly published novels, poems and theological essays. He gave organ recitals. During summer vacations he ministered to small village congregations that needed his service.

To be sure they were keenly aware of the fact that their new homeland, Hungary, fought the war on Hitler's side. Prominent Hungarian politicians attempted to force the Hungarian government to pull out of the war and desert Nazi Germany, but they were doomed to failure. His country was marching toward the abyss. Meanwhile, Imre reached what he thought to be the first achievement of his career, the *summa cum laude* diploma from the Unitarian Theological Academy of Kolozsvár in July, 1943.

It was only now that he finally let his life's real dream go, that of studying medicine. His parallel studies at two different universities had concealed an intellectual anesthesia against the pain of his assumption that the noble profession of medicine had been unreachable for a poor boy like him. He had never revolted against poverty. In fact, he had accepted it with a self-righteous dignity. His class identity was deeply engraved in his personality. His whole being was molded around his peasant core. Although his education and intellectual achievements elevated him to a high social rank, he could never overcome his sense of inferiority in the society of the elite. He attributed to them virtues and admirable qualities, always above his own. Now he had to concede that poverty had scarred him by blocking his access to the realm of medicine.

* * *

His intellectual thriving bought an added dimension, a friendship that weighed as much in importance as his achievements. He found a master, Dr. Dániel Simén, the professor of practical theology, and the master found him. Imre wanted nothing but to sit at his feet forever. He expressed his devotion to him in the language of odes. Dr. Simén was greatly respected for being one of the few Unitarian theologians to study at the Pacific School of Theology in Berkeley, California. He carried an atmosphere of superiority. Even his rivals agreed—and they were numerous—that he was one of the Church's most brilliant orators. He was twenty-five years elder to Imre, as well as to his wife, the beautiful Aranka. Imre became a family confidant during his years of seminary and beyond. His self-confidence blossomed under their nurturing attention.

Imre's exclusive loyalty blinded him and blocked any other prospects for social connections. It also veiled his mentor's character traits, which, according to his opponents, varied from vanity to ruthless arrogance. At that time Dr. Simén was the vice-Bishop of the Unitarian Church and had a fierce ambition to win the position of the only Unitarian bishop in the world. He had all the qualities of a head of a church, except humility. He was utterly unpopular, but he seemed to ignore it. Imre was in total denial of it. Simén was his role model and he was willing to lay down his life for his master—and in a sense, he did later, more than metaphorically.

Freshly graduated, Imre and his colleagues eagerly awaited their first assignments as interns, a two-year practicum. The two prospective churches couldn't have been more different: Budapest's Unitarian Mission House and Székelykeresztúr's Unitarian college. Matching the church with the intern seemed to be straightforward. Imre, considered "the star" of the Seminary, would obviously be placed in the capital of Hungary. At this threshold, however, the inner insecurity of the village boy surfaced in panic. His immediate argument for rejection of Budapest was his doubts about his capacity to live up to the challenges of Europe's great cultural center. He had visited Budapest only once before and found it dazzling. It was precisely its splendor that now frightened him. Besides, he stayed firmly committed to village ministry. It didn't even occur to him to compare himself to a classmate of modest intellectual caliber. He simply asked him to consider swapping their assignments. In disbelief, the classmate accepted the offer, and Imre took the little college town close to his birthplace.

From time to time, colleagues predicted that Imre would become the Bishop of the Unitarian Church. "God dropped Imre on this earth earmarked," they would say. Who would have believed then that his classmate would end up as a bishop much later in Hungary while Imre would begin a journey into oblivion?

CHAPTER 2

The War Loses its Sting

I mre Gellérd arrived at his new post in the Unitarian College of Székelykeresztúr in November, 1943. Although this was a time of uncertainty in the midst of the chaos of war, Imre's youthful enthusiasm turned his attention toward loftier pursuits. The "ambitious teacher" in him had found a needy yet operational college after all. One of the most desired Unitarian pulpits in Transylvania was now his, and he became the sole minister to the neighboring parishes as well. Dean Lajos Ütö and other ministers from the neighboring villages had fled the war, and these congregations desperately needed to hear messages of hope and meaning. Imre's churches filled Sunday after Sunday, and not just with Unitarians. He was loved. He was needed. For him the war lost its sting.

The College of Székelykeresztúr [Cristurul Secuiesc], the second greatest Unitarian learning center after Kolozsvár, also warmly welcomed him. Most of the teachers had also fled the war zone, but most of the students had remained. Rich teaching opportunities opened for Imre. He taught psychology, philosophy, French and Romanian, in addition to carrying out the duties of his original appointment as supervisor/educator/spiritual advisor to the College's boarding school for students who traditionally came from surrounding villages. The school's nineteenth-century benefactor Baron Balázs Orbán had endowed the school with enough resources to continue educating the poor but talented village children of the Székelyland. Younger teachers such as Imre were housed with the students, sharing living space as well as lifestyle choices and personal interactions. This system resulted in the formation of strong bonds between students and faculty, and it fostered an environment for intense learning and a strong sense of community.

The school rightly boasted of many renowned intellectuals among its alumni. One in particular was Ferenc Balázs, the great writer and Unitarian minister of Mészkö, the "Alabaster Village." After finishing his studies at Oxford, England, and Berkeley, California, Balázs traveled around the world to meet liberal co-religionists. Upon returning to Transylvania, he was first assigned in Székelykeresztúr, to the same job Imre now held, where he was the first to champion modern social changes in Transylvania's villages. He died tragically of tuberculosis at age thirty-six in 1937. Imre thus stepped into the legacy of his highly admired role model.

Imre almost immediately began to implement his freshly acquired pedagogical and psychological methods. The entire school became an unprecedented experimental laboratory of advanced pedagogy. His students published a new literary journal, *Kévekötés* [*Sheaving*], containing original poems and short novels by students and teachers. In the midst of the fear, lethargy and hopelessness of the times, this group of starving students and teachers, this hardy little band of radical social activists, formed a nearly ideal spiritual community. It was this kind of reality which Imre dreamed into being.

The City Lost its Innocence

In March, 1944, Imre was appointed to be a permanent teacher in the Unitarian College of Székelykeresztúr. That same month, Germany occupied Hungary. News from the battle front was alarming, but it always seemed removed and distant. That is, until one night when, in this peaceful little town, the unthinkable happened: the deportation of Jews began. Rumors about deportations had circulated earlier, but they seemed absurd. After all, Székelykeresztúr had become a thriving center of culture and commerce mainly because of its large Jewish population. Most of the shops were Jewish property. Cultured, kind and elegant, the Jews belonged intimately to the fabric of that society. If there was any cosmopolitan air in the city, it was because of them. When the reality of deportations hit full force, people froze with unanswered questions. Why had the Jews not been warned about the impending danger? How could they have been so surprised and so unprepared? What should they have anticipated, to be prepared for? How could such a disgrace fall upon their town and other towns all over Transylvania? How could the citizens have allowed their neighbors and friends to be kidnapped under cover of night without even hearing it? One third of the high school students—those bright, beautiful teenagers, so full of promise—simply vanished! Imre lived far from the main road and learned about the catastrophe the morning after.

What could be done? Outbursts of indignation were swiftly muted with the chilly warning, "Anyone who shows signs of sympathy or solidarity with the Jews will share their fate!" The shops remained closed. The people of Székelykeresztúr did not dare to come out of their houses. A suffocating black cloud engulfed them. Guilt, fear and shame tormented them. With the loss of their Jews, the community had lost its innocence and its dignity.

Imre had not been aware of open anti-Semitism before in Székelykeresztúr or elsewhere. But this area of Transylvania now belonged to Hungary, a *fascist* country, and thus had unwittingly become Germany's accomplice. Transylvanians now learned firsthand about the terror of the Hungarian *gendarmes*—the savages of Adolf Eichmann and the fascist *Nyilas* party–which had overtaken their mother country.

During these days of darkness, one man, Áron Márton, the Roman Catholic Bishop of Transylvania, with extraordinary integrity and courage, rose to be a beacon in saving Christian honor from total dehumanization. In May, 1944, he preached his famous sermon on the Holocaust in St. Michael Cathedral of Kolozsvár at the height of the deportation of Jews. In it Bishop Áron—people affectionately called him by his first name— openly condemned anti-Semitism. He praised Roman Catholics and Protestants alike who demonstrated their support of the victims, and he further called for solidarity among all Christians and Jews. He urged the people of Transylvania to take a moral stand against Nazism in the name of Christ, human rights and human dignity. He called upon the governments of Romania and Hungary to exercise their power to stop the mass murder of deported Jews. Bishop Áron's call helped to shake many from fear, including two Unitarian bishops, Bishop Miklós Józan of Kolozsvár and Sándor Szent Iványi, deputy Bishop of Hungary, who forged birth certificates to save many lives.

August 23, 1944, brought a dramatic change in the political arena and in the personal lives of Transylvanians. Romania suddenly joined the Allied Forces. Until then, Romania and Hungary had been "allies" in the Germans' venomous grip. Now they suddenly became mortal enemies. The joint German and Hungarian army launched a last desperate attack against Romania and Southern Transylvania. Hungary, out of an ominous sense of honor, stubbornly and tragically stayed loyal to Hitler, and Transylvania became the battlefield between the Nazis and the Russian Red Army. The very structure of life seemed to collapse in those days. The heat of that summer, a persistent +38 degrees Celsius, mimed an apocalyptic atmosphere. Imre's neighborhood became the site of ferocious crossfire between the Germans and Russians. Confused and scared, he decided to flee to his mother's home 30 kilometers away. Traveling as fast as he could, he met an old friend on the road. "What should I do?" he impatiently questioned this good man. The friend said, "This is the wrong direction to flee. You will be caught in front line crossfire or perhaps worse, become a prisoner of war. Turn around! Go back!" Imre soon learned just how God-sent this advice was, and he escaped both injury and capture.[1]

"We Either Win Him Over or Destroy Him"

Socialist-communist ideas to a young idealist represented an exciting intellectual challenge. To Imre such ideas pertained to the Christian social principles of a just society, and he therefore embraced them. How could he or anyone else have predicted that the very people who helped the new ideals penetrate society would later become communism's victims? As the only expert in Marxism-Leninism, Imre was in great demand as a speaker. His somewhat underground lectures—he received death threats from time to time—were increasingly popular, especially among the youth. The way he portrayed his vision of Christian socialism and its compatibility

---

[1]According to official history, the Red Army liberated Romania from Nazi occupation. Later, as a result of the Second Treaty of Vienna, the borders of Transylvania were moved again, for good, back to the post-Trianon state. Hungarians in Transylvania became Romanian citizens once again. According to the Vienna Treaty the United Nations Charter guaranteed respect for human rights, with a special stipulation for religious and cultural rights for minorities in the new Romania. True equality was also guaranteed in the Romanian Constitution. In Fall, 1944, the new Romanian government issued a solemn proclamation that reinforced of the principle of equal rights for all citizens of Romania. At the same time, however, it launched vehement attacks against Transylvanian Hungarians. Violating the Charter's principles, Romanian nationalist militia troops carried out pogroms in Hungarian villages, like one at Szárazajta. In October, 1944, thousands of Hungarian men between the age fifteen and fifty-five were randomly rounded up on the streets of Kolozsvár, deported, tortured and kept in forced labor camps in the Ural mountains in the Soviet Union. About seven hundred died there of infectious diseases and starvation. Imre's beloved theology professor, Dr. János Erdö, was among those captured one morning as he walked from his home to the Seminary. His escape, and how he jumped out of the cattle train carrying him to the labor camp, and how he walked home from Russia, hiding in Russian villages, was a hero's story.

It was Bishop Áron Márton once again who, while assuming that the Vatican's power and authority was behind him, openly condemned the renewed oppression of the country's Hungarian minorities. Unfortunately, he soon recognized the painful reality that Rome's principal concern was the expansion of the Catholic Church, not the oppression of ethnic minorities, even if they were Roman Catholics.

with the gospel message, found sympathetic ears with his colleagues and students. His liberal Unitarian Church embraced these social ideas. He was often reminded about being predestined to become the theoretician of the new socialist movement. He became active in the newly founded Association of Young Communists. Soon he found himself involved with the electoral campaign of Dr. Petru Groza's first communist government. Representing the Hungarian League of Nations, Imre was their keynote speaker on behalf of the Hungarian minorities.

His local political activity and popularity among the Hungarian minorities, as well as his education in the Romanian language—the official language of the country to which Transylvania now belonged—resulted in the stunning offer of a political career. The newly formed Romanian communist government of Dr. Groza invited Imre to join it as a member of the Central Committee, to represent the country's minorities.

This opportunity presented Imre with the most agonizing dilemma of his life. It seemed to be a monumental career advancement that coincidentally afforded the wherewithal to serve his people. His ambition was already pushing him toward the desire for power. The position did not seem like selfish careerism, for it was about service to others. His friends' verdict was, "You are the right person at the right time, so go for it!" but that only tormented him. He must have known on some level that his choice would have irrevocable consequences. He groped about to find good reasons to back off. He could come up with only one sound counter-argument, namely, that his Christian ministry would be in conflict with communist atheism. This excuse did not have much merit at that time, for communism was full of promises of the highest social ideals, and Imre was ultimately committed to those. While the inherent possibilities in this position would provide influence over minority policy-making, it would also turn into an imperative of responsibility. While he desired power, he feared the change which that power could bring.

Ultimately, his inner sense of insecurity came to his "rescue," paralyzing him. First his body revolted. His migraine headaches became unbearable. He fell seriously ill with pleurisy, which was feared to be of tubercular origin. The current postwar economic depression, the near-starvation throughout the country, and the lack of medicine all foreshadowed grim prospects. He was bedridden and isolated for months, which surely dulled his optimism and skewed his perspective. All the while he procrastinated over making a final decision and hid his anxiety about making a change as radical as leaving the intimacy of a college town and moving to the Romanian capitol, Bucharest.

Finally, his answer was *no*. Yet, his decision did not bring him relief. His ambivalence persisted. His missed chance became his tormentor. He fully realized the potential faultiness of his choice when a former student, modest in talents but astute politically, seized the position that his teacher had rejected.

Soon after, at an infamous meeting at the county Party headquarters, it was said, "We either win Imre Gellérd to our side, or we destroy him."

The choice was still in Imre's hands. He could have reversed his decision, but he was unaware that he could. In the moment of his decision he could only see the high ideals of the Communist Party. Later, witnessing their distortion into totalitarianism under his former student's direction, he wondered about his own willingness for compromises, open confrontations, and public humiliations of helplessness–all part of the very nature of that job. How far could have he gone in being coopted and coerced to betray his integrity? How would his leadership abilities have had the desired impact on a national level in a hostile nationalistic atmosphere?

The moment he rejected the invitation to power, he set into motion the political mechanism of his own annihilation.

CHAPTER 3

In Love

I mplicit in Imre's career decision was choosing the church and choosing to minister to those faithful to the soil in the villages. Following his ordination as a minister by the Unitarian Synod held in Székelykeresztúr on September 15, 1946, and following his graduation from Bolyai University in the same year, his vision had a chance to blossom fully. His spirit soared high in spite of the widening famine. He had a college and a city whose citizens expected their spirit and intellect to be nurtured. His ultimate goal was nothing less than to reform and renew his church in its theology, liturgy and spirituality. The obvious path to take was that of his great pre-war predecessor Rev. Ferencz Balázs. Imre assumed that challenge in his efforts to rekindle the same spark in his work toward social transformation.

Imre could not have found a more responsive audience for his renewal plan than his students. One of the brightest among them was a young woman named Judit Kovács. He glimpsed her for the first time from the pulpit in 1944. She was Roman Catholic, yet she began to show up for Unitarian services. Elegant and reserved, passionate yet unapproachable, Judit was a phenomenon in the town. Her beauty enchanted many. She was eighteen. Imre secretly fell in love with her, but social obstacles rendered it nearly impossible to approach her for a long time. Eventually, though, he found some ways.

First, he became her teacher, an arguable blessing. It was as much a delight to him as a discomfort to perform in her presence, in the fire of her searching eyes. There were few social occasions for them to meet outside of school boundaries, for Judit was guarded by a seven-headed dragon, her stepmother. Judit did not attend school-sponsored events such as the popular hiking trips, poetry recitals or choir singing. She played the piano beautifully but her stepmother never allowed her to perform in school. Her infatuated male classmates tried to bypass her mother and get her attention, but she was always busy with tutoring students until late in the evening. Even during Easters when all the boys paid a "ritual" visit to all the girls—the "sprinkling spree"—Judit's gate was locked. Her eyes red from crying, she looked longingly at her many disappointed visitors from behind closed windows.

Finally they met at a school ball. They danced through the night—in the presence of her guarding stepmother. No longer able to keep his secret, he declared his love for her, and that immediately complicated their professional life. Though he was her teacher, he openly and properly courted her. Judit seemed to reciprocate his feelings, but also important was that her stepmother accepted him without reservation. As a college teacher and a celebrated preacher in the town, his social status was as high as it could rise, but he still felt miserably inferior and awkward in Judit's elegant, middle-class environment. He considered himself a pariah, with his meager salary, no place of his own, and no material possessions except his books. He nevertheless became obsessed with her.

If Imre wanted to possess her for her beauty and poise before he knew her dark secrets, he soon wished to save her, but not without some confusion of his roles as suitor, minister and teacher.

Princess in Captivity—Judit's Saga

"My earliest memory," Judit began her story, "is one of a speeding train in front of our house, and I am running toward it. Our elderly neighbor snatched me. I cried out, "Why? I want to die!"

I had been waiting for my mother to come home. I wore the same dress year in and year out, every day since she had left. It used to be black, but I cried it into gray. It all started with black vultures invading our house, kidnapping my mother in a casket. They covered it with flowers, so I could not see her. I wished I could have looked at her a little longer, but they nailed the lid. "Poor orphans!" Their whispers and cries disturbed me. My father had died the year before, my sister told me. I was afraid the same would happen to my mother despite her strong assurance that she would never leave me. She loved me and I believed her.

With our mother gone I and my two brothers, aged twelve and fourteen, were left in the care of our older sister, aged sixteen. Our uncle, the appointed guardian, was a brutal man. He gave us more beatings than meals. He fleeced us of our beautiful house and our farmland, the Szilas, and gave us four children up for adoption. We lost our home in Székelykeresztúr.

Our oldest sister Ilona left for Bucharest to earn her living as a maid, as was customary for Székely girls of her age. I, a five-year-old, was left with a family who offered me room and board, seasoned with plenty of beatings. What I dreaded most was my being chained to the big kitchen table every time they left home. Hours of crying made me unbearably thirsty, but the thirst did not go away by drinking water. I shivered but I was cold from the inside.

My name was Juliska Bakó, which must have stood for unhappy child. I decided that Juliska must die, whatever "dying" would mean. I wanted to be no longer, like my mother. An absent child could not be brutalized. Unfortunately, I failed in my will. The old man rescued me from the train. I was utterly disappointed, but it eventually precipitated change. Our neighbors immediately found a good foster family for me, and my sister sent me packages of crumbled cookies from Bucharest.

In the summer of 1933 everything turned around. An elegant, middle-aged couple visited us. They paid unusual attention to me, talking about me all the time.

"She is charming," the lady said, "I want her." I was six years old then. A few weeks later I found myself in a nice home, which was now mine. I was adopted. I was their "first-born," my new father boasted. On that day the peasant name Juliska died, and the more elegant name Judit was given to me. The new Judit belonged to Zsuzsanna and János Kovács. I loved my metamorphosis. It came with lots of attention, kisses and hugs, a beautiful new dress, and neighbors' visits. We had pork and cabbage for lunch that day and we prayed at the table. The best was yet to come, when in a few weeks my father, a handsome, tall gentleman took me to school for the first time. We had a piano, and soon I took piano lessons from an unpleasant old lady.

At first I was suspicious of so much happiness. All they expected from me was obedience. Mother often reminded me that this obligation was made in return for being saved from orphanhood. This was an unnecessary worry on her part, for I had no other wish but to please her at any cost. I enjoyed school, and I got the highest grades without much effort. I befriended the nicest girls in my class. They usually spent the afternoons together and invited me along. I had never had friends or toys before, and the desire to play overwhelmed me. But my mother severely curtailed my freedom, and she didn't welcome my friends to our house either.

She gave me mounds of duties every day. I hated washing dishes, but it was still the easiest job. The faster I worked to be free and play, the more the tasks multiplied. The sweet new home gradually transformed into captivity.

Mother, as I was supposed to call her, was a recognized artist of handicrafts. We had our own shop in the main square of the town where she sold her own creations, from fancy embroidery and lace to hats and Persian style rugs.

I was now ten years old and already trained in most needlework. Once, mother gave me a deadline to finish a 3 by 5 meter lace curtain, then left for shopping in the neighboring town. My father and I shared a great distress over this impossible task. He had to build me a platform, putting a chair on top of the table, and he held me up so I could reach the top of the lace that reached from the floor to the ceiling. My specialty was petit point goblin tapestry. One single piece would take months of intense work.

I never dared to think that I was close to being enslaved. I never called my mother a "stepmother." I simply acknowledged life as continual work if one wanted to be respectable. My attempts at defiance were severely punished by mother, but at least I knew the reason for the beatings. Punishment came sweetly packaged along with my gentle father's comforting words. His solidarity made suffering worthwhile.

The child in me wanted to stay a child at any cost. My stepmother gave me beautiful dolls and a doll house for the first Christmas, but I was forbidden to play with them. I was supposed to admire them from afar. It was sheer agony. So I came up with an idea: I told my mother that our teacher expected the girls to take their dolls to school for a doll exhibition. For a long while these sweet stolen hours of playing remained undetected, but eventually my dolls were stolen from school.

My school organized hiking trips each fall, iceskating during the winter, and dance parties in between. All my friends were present at these joyous occasions except me. The more my friends begged Mother on my behalf, the more resistant she became to letting me go. Crushed and heartbroken, the princess in disguise dreamed of a miraculous intervention while working obediently, endlessly. Even movies, especially movies, were taboo for me. But I could not resist that temptation. I ended up seeing every movie, illegally of course, during school time. My teachers were quite aware of my "strict upbringing" and they allied with me, covering up for the movie sessions and even for an occasional school party.

Judit's story increased Imre's determination to save her. His mandate in life was to take her away from it all. It turned out that Judit's parents played a key role in solidifying his goal. They told him, "You cannot be a Communist activist and see our daughter at the same time." Imre's choice was thus propitiatory not only toward Judit's revealed tribulations but also by his rejection of a political career. Her story continued.

Mother seemed to enjoy inflicting me with her extreme mood swings. For no apparent reason she suddenly displayed resentment and anger toward me, blaming me for something I did not feel responsible for. She would not even talk to me for days at a time. I panicked that I would lose her love. I cried my eyes out, begging for forgiveness, although I had no idea what precipitated the crisis. I accused myself because she did. Then just as suddenly she declared forgiveness. Being taken back into her grace overwhelmed me with happiness, but these frequent rituals emotionally exhausted me. Father quietly suffered along with me, but he was too afraid to intervene.

The more punishments I got, the more I retreated into my fantasy world, coming up with the most elaborate lies for the sake of a little freedom. In the end, though, I voluntarily admitted my guilt and surrendered to the punishment. Beatings were merely daily routine. What I considered to be real agony was being locked into the cellar at night. There were mice down there for which I had a phobia. Over time the mice grew into rats in my recurring nightmares. Mother loved to scare me, and when I broke down, she was pleased and rewarded me.

The ultimate punishment game was called "the bag," which featured being "fired" as her daughter. With this pastime she would break my heart over and over. With a small bag containing my belongings, she put me out on the street and locked the gate behind me. "We've had enough of you," she said. "Find another home." I wanted to vanish in shame, to be devoured by the very earth in my grief. I did not dare to cry, for I would have been given extra punishment for embarrassing her in front of the neighbors. Finally, late at night, upon Father's intervention, forgiveness would be bestowed upon me. For a few days we would be exuberant, and I tried ever so hard to be the girl she wanted. During those good days she was generous and genuinely loving. She sewed beautiful dresses for me and cooked my favorite meals.

One day mother informed me that she and my father had been placed under a curse by a Gypsy sorceress, who had hidden the witchcraft under our apple tree. Unless she found it, they would live under its spell. The curse was responsible for alienating her husband from her.

"Therefore," she reminded me, "you are God's gift to comfort me." Her words both touched me and weighed heavily on my conscience. I was ready to comfort my unhappy mother and bring joy into her life, whatever that would mean.

It meant horror. I did not have my own bed, and I slept in the matrimonial bed at Mother's side. Piles of pillows separated the two of us. Her physical closeness at first felt reassuring to the child so eager to be loved. Then, one day, mother forced me to "play" with her. I did not dare scream. I obeyed then and ever after, for this was my duty.

My stepmother was desperate to break the power of the witchcraft responsible for their failed marriage. The witchcraft supposedly was implanted within the property of the target person as a tangible substance, such as a bunch of hemp or a piece of rug. Someone with an equal shamanic power was able to release the person from under the spell only by removing its vehicle. Over the years our entire life revolved around her obsession. She hired Gypsy women and Romanian Orthodox priests to undo the curse. These "employees" literally ruined us financially, extorting more and more reward for their services. Mother gave away not only the family savings, but occasionally our very food and personal belongings. The police had to intervene a few times. When I grew older and spoke Romanian, Mother took me on her trips to a far-away Romanian Orthodox monastery where she hoped to find help. I dreaded these long and menacing trips across the Fogaras mountains to the Brincoveanu monastery. We had to stay there overnight under the gaze of those long-bearded monks.

The arsenal of abuses kept widening. Close to bankruptcy and desperate, mother found a new obsession: occultism. Now thirteen, I was forced to play the role of the medium as she practiced necromancy. For long and scary hours of the night, I was ordered to assist in contacting the spirits of the dead and "finding out" bloody secrets about the family, such as who killed her father. Since she ignored my resentment, in retaliation I decided to manipulate the "spirits." I made up dramatic statements and messages "from beyond." We used the technique of walking a coin in front of the alphabet, trying to read the message as the coin moved from letter to letter. The medium's finger, mine, was supposed to gently touch the coin and just follow its movement. When my sleep deprivation grew serious, I "sent" a message to my mother through her late father. One night I made the coin read, "My dear daughter, you have violated me, and now I have to stand before God. If you try to invoke me ever again, you will get such a headache that you will know God's anger toward you." Indeed, when my addicted mother started the next séance, she broke down with a violent headache. What scared me then was my own intuited power over her. I did not dare use it, though; she still had total control over me.

"Addicted to abuse, she can be liberated only by my unconditional love!" Imre thought with a growing tenacity of will, as he listened to the distressing saga.

Mother had hallucinations and visions of religious content. She would wake me up during the night to describe her visions. Her descriptions were so suggestive that sometimes I had the impression that I saw them. I would never question their reality to my mother. These phenomena of light took different forms. A recurring vision which appeared between the mirror and our bed was of Jesus riding a donkey surrounded by "heavenly light." My mother was transfixed by its beauty. Sleepy and scared, I had to watch and see it too. Having a vivid fantasy, it was not difficult to please her. So we discussed the "details" of the vision, while I tried to hang onto my sanity.

As a teenager I was often reminded how beautiful I was. My wardrobe, mostly my own knitting, was considered elegant. I began to notice how boys in our class reacted to my appearance. When mother decided that I was about to fall in love with a classmate—a teenager!—she curtailed my socializing opportunities even further. She despised boys of my age. I had a few handsome schoolmates who tried in vain to break through the barriers of my prison and free me. An enchanted princess, the seven-headed dragon, fierce knights–my youth was a romantic one.

My alleged beauty brought more disaster upon me. My stepmother invited grown-up men to our home and encouraged them to court me. I was ordered to be–"kind" to them. When I was thirteen or fourteen a fat salesman stayed in our home for days. It was my duty to take his meals into his room. He showed me a bunch of money, promising to give it to me if I let him "touch" me. Horrified, I ran away, preferring to take my mother's punishment. Later an army officer paid me regular visits at my mother's invitation. She wanted to push me into his arms at age sixteen. Like a tiger I fought for my dear honor.

My own miseries were soon overshadowed by the outbreak of war. It would have remained an abstract evil for me had I not lost my best friend Pálma Dávid. She was Jewish. We had vowed lifelong friendship to each other, sealing it with our very blood. I was loved by her family of three generations, all kind, intelligent people. I could have never before imagined a family so loving and devoted to each other. I sat at their Passover table and I longed to belong there. I was proud of my Jewish name Judit.

One day my parents forbade me to visit them. The yellow star was placed on their house. They are dangerous, I was told. My best friend, dangerous? Defiantly I went to their house anyway. Mrs. Dávid burst out crying when she saw me. "You will live, you will have a family and children. But who knows what will happen to my daughters?" she wailed. She immediately realized the irrationality of her outburst and hugged me. "Go away," she sobbed. "It is dangerous for you to be with us. You must live. Be careful, and never come to our house again. We love you, so we want to protect you. Go!" Shame and guilt crashed upon me in that moment. I wanted to apologize and do something for them. I was one with them. Then Pálma, with a strange solemnity in her voice, said to me, "We are God's people. If God calls us to lay down our lives, we will do it. Our people will always be in God's hands." Her face lit up with an unearthly passion. At that moment she looked like an angel.

I ran sobbing to the neighboring shop and asked what was going to happen to the Jews. A man whom I didn't know grabbed me. "Crying, crying because of the filthy Jews, heh? Go and join them!" He spanked me so hard that I landed on my face in the street.

A few nights later I woke up as if by an earthquake. Fourteen large horse carts filled with the Jews of our town and the neighboring villages were leaving town in a long procession in front of our house. My best friend Pálma was among them! She was engaged, and her wedding with a Hungarian man would have been soon. She was already pregnant. Another woman Mrs. Kain huddled with her two babies; her loud crying broke my heart. I felt a powerful urge to join them, but my spark of humanity was overcome by fear.

Years later they learned that out of Székelykeresztúr's large Jewish population, only two survived Auschwitz: the handsome Sándor Gidáli and Lili Dávid, Pálma's sister. Pálma gave birth to her baby in the death camp. They were both killed in Auschwitz's gas chambers, along with the other seven members of her family.

"I believed I would never again be able to forge deep friendships," Judit confessed as she continued to reflect on her ordeals during the war.

In summer, 1944 , the front moved to our very backyard. Gun battles raged around our town as Russian troops replaced the Germans. In part because I was in real danger of being raped, my parents decided it was time to flee the town. With the roar of cannon shots all around us we did not have time to pack. Under cover of night we took off on foot, trying to reach the remote village of Solymos [Soimosul Mare], the place of my stepparents' ancestry. We met German troops on our way, who warned us about some entrenched Russians in the very direction we were heading.

We had to pass through the battlefront—there was no other way. That was the longest night of my life. Caught in the crossfire between Germans and Russians, we heard shells flying over our heads in both directions as we crawled through the line. As unbelievable as it seemed, we traversed the twelve kilometers safely and arrived at my uncle's home by morning, only to learn that Russians had already occupied the village and looted some of the houses. They were looking for watches and women, but they took anything in between. Now I was in even greater danger. My aunt used the old method of disguising me as an old woman and ordered me to hide. My hiding places varied between the chicken coop and the pig barn. I rarely dared to sleep in the house. One time my uncle lowered me deep down into their well, but I was more terrified of that "safety." From my hiding places I often watched the soldiers searching the house and yard. I held my breath and prayed to be invisible.

The fighting finally died out and we rushed back home to Székelykeresztúr. We found our house undamaged. All we lost was my dowry, the precious collection that I had embroidered. I could not imagine what possible use a combat soldier would have for the fine linen. We found pieces of lace littered in the mud, but I could not have cared less after going through hell. It took that night between the front lines to make us realize how little our material possessions really matter. Life—life is the only treasure. And I had it!

Ambivalence of Destiny

Judit finished up her studies one year early, taking a double load and graduating from the Unitarian college in 1946. Imre finally pulled his strength together and proposed to her. It was then that Judit revealed her last secret, her life's dream. In response, Imre's incessant self-ambivalence gushed forth once again. He wrote her this letter in sheer madness:

My Dear Judit,

My soul is overflowing with grief as if facing death. This world is alien to me. The desire to return to my simple roots tempts me once again. I can only think in extremes: either to choose the nameless simplicity of a peasant's life with all its earthiness, or to become powerful and shine. I want millions to depend on me while I create the conditions for their happiness. I cannot bare mediocrity.

My ill-fated decision brought me to this situation and it tears me apart. I am fully aware that what I am proposing to you will ruin both of us. My burning, pure, blessed love for you tries to gain justification in the shadow of life's other realities. Poor Judit! How God can be so cruel toward you to send me into your life— the man who cannot be happy! I had always felt too small, too insignificant for you. You deserve so much more than I can be. I have sinned against you.

In my dream you were my wife, beautiful, painfully beautiful, like in reality. But I was not happy. We were standing before a mirror that reflected our souls and I read our future. You were suffering in my dream. Your friends married professors with fame. I realized that I was an obstacle in your career and fulfillment. You are so intelligent, and your prospective options are so brilliant. Your happiness lies in your calling, in your career. I see you as a medical doctor, mastering the profession that had been also my dream; but it was out of my reach. Today you confessed your secret, your real desire, your true calling: to become a physician!

I met you this morning. You were so beautiful, so elegant. There was so much desire in your eyes, such hidden energies, ready to break loose. Your personality demands fame, power, wealth. I look at your home; it is so elegant and I am so awkward in it. You are too beautiful for me.

Dear Judit, I have realized that I must make up for my terrible mistake, I must let you go. I clearly see that I am a hindrance to your self-fulfillment. It is my moral duty to act as your former teacher and urge you, carry on your dream! Your place is at a university. I feel responsible before God for your future and happiness. If social prejudices allowed, I would give half of my income toward your education, to see you blossom and become a doctor for our suffering people. I would urge you to marry someone who is worthier than I am to be your husband.

I will try to avoid you. I am very ill with pneumonia right now and very lonely. I don't know what my future holds. But I must get out of your way. My mother keeps asking me, "Do you think Judit would marry you if you asked her? And if you became a minister, wouldn't she be embarrassed to be a preacher's wife? Did you think through, my dear son, that she is too delicate, too beautiful a young woman for the miseries of village life? Could she face it? Would she want it?" My own mother is more worried about you than about me. We are not the family you want and deserve. We have been broken and I am a victim of our miserable past.

I will help you get through our separation and breakup—while I rebel against God, for letting us pay for love with so much pain. Yet we must not become victims of love.

Please, absolve me from my sin of weakness and irresponsibility toward you. Life owes you more than I am or can be.

Yours, Imre.

Judit's response to this letter came in the form of action. She summoned all her courage, fled her home, and enrolled in the same school, Bolyai University in Kolozsvár. She began her studies in mathematics and physics, but she did not stay there long. The new medical school at Marosvásárhely [Tirgu Mures] had just opened, and not hesitating to step onto the path of her true calling, she transferred there immediately. They were still engaged but she stopped writing him. Her parents, however, were committed to keep their relationship alive. Her stepmother assured Imre that Judit would marry him. This perspective nurtured his burning desire for her, even while he knew that he should set his butterfly free, out of love.

Imre finally gathered his courage again and visited Judit at the medical school. She was thriving—ranked first in her class and more beautiful than ever—but she was aloof and reluctant to spend more than a short hour in the school's garden with him. He staggered home to his dormitory in Székelykeresztúr, promising himself to give up on her.

He didn't. He couldn't.

When Judit finally came home for spring vacation during her second year at medical school, her parents arranged their marriage! They all assured Judit that her medical studies would in no way be interrupted by the marriage. How did the strong-willed Judit accept this fate? Let her say in her own words:

I was free. I was to become a doctor! I was in love.

The long, dark years of the war that robbed us of our youth now gave way to an ebullient, insatiable thirst for life. The thin boundary between life and death in the operating room overwhelmed me with an urge to live faster, fuller. Love so pure, so unambiguous, burst into my full-of-taboos life. I finally discovered life at nineteen. My chosen prince was a classmate, an Armenian. The promise of happiness was so rich, so reachable.

It seemed as if my newly found love swept away my impenetrable, built-in guilt mechanisms. Three semesters passed before I came home again to my parents and Imre in 1947. In the presence of years of abuse, my illusory freedom suddenly collapsed. My mother's suspicious, penetrating eyes destroyed my self-confidence and triggered a fatal confession. I asked for her approval of my new love.

Mother was outraged. For her, being in love was immoral. She was threatened with losing her "asset," my virginity. I was still her exclusive property. "You will become a virtuous housewife, not an immoral doctor! Medicine is promiscuous," was her final pronouncement.

Imre stubbornly believed that Judit was *his* destiny and justified it with a conviction that she loved him.

Sobbing Bride

On Pentecost, 1947, the jubilant town and college witnessed Judit and Imre's wedding in the Unitarian church where he served. Judit sobbed through the ceremony; Imre was exalted. Something else happened to Judit besides her wedding on that day.

I was Roman Catholic by birth and my stepparents were devout Calvinists, but they respected my faith and encouraged me to practice it. I had attended Roman Catholic church and Sunday school. I held my faith in the center of my life. Just before the marriage ceremony I was unexpectedly asked to sign a document that "automatically" converted me to Unitarianism, a precondition to marrying a Unitarian clergyman. It never occurred to me that I would be marrying a minister. Imre, after all, was a college teacher. My doubts about our fast-track marriage, my inflicted sense of guilt about my coerced apostasy, my fear of mother's revenge for my reluctance—all these feelings weighed heavily against the excitement of a girl marrying an admired and accomplished scholar, writer, poet and teacher. I went ahead and signed the document. I was envied in the town. I anticipated bliss in the unknown of marriage. I loved Imre intellectually if not physically.

We spent our first night together in the college dormitory. It was filled with white lilies. Their heavy fragrance was a sweet poison in the small room and almost turned our matrimonial bed into a catafalque.

How thin is the boundary between life and death, between bliss and agony.

Imre was now a young husband and too happy to worry about his poverty. In the great post-war depression his monthly salary was barely enough for their daily bread. Village ministry became the obvious solution. With the sudden death of the minister in Siménfalva, a village only seven kilometers away, this prestigious pulpit became available. Imre moved into the elegant parsonage and was able to keep his teaching job too. At Thanksgiving (September) of 1947 a happy man and his beautiful wife arrived at Siménfalva in a horse cart. Imre's installation at the church of Siménfalva marked the beginning of his dreams' fulfillment and the shattering of Judit's. There was no precedent for a minister's wife to spend five years away from her husband in school. Moreover, Judit quickly became pregnant. She thus ended up sacrificing her medical career under all kinds of social expectations and pressures. She never openly rebelled at her situation, and Imre was blinded by his own happiness. They both glowed in their own idealism, but Imre failed to recognize that Judit's aspirations and goals were different from his. He wanted to believe that they were a perfect couple, as did everybody around them.

Sowing and Reaping

For the next twelve years they evolved together into what people called "living legends." Siménfalva was an idyllic place in the Nyikó valley called "the pearl of the Nyikó." As Imre's congregation gained considerable status, it became known as "the pearl of the Unitarian Church." Judit shared all of his professional and social roles with her husband. She grew into a community leader who was respected and even adored. She seemed to adjust perfectly to village conditions, largely because her role was so full of meaning. Yet deep down, Imre knew that she would never come to terms with giving up her own career. This was not her life; she was living her husband's, gracefully.

College teaching kept Imre away from home a lot, especially at the beginning of their marriage. Judit carried the workload of the large household and carried out the obligations to the community, but she insisted on teaching mathematics at the local school. They needed this extra income and she enjoyed teaching. Until the very hour of delivery of her first child, she was up and working hard.

It was unfortunate that Imre missed their daughter's birth. That day, March 15, 1948, was the Hungarian national holiday celebrating the 100th anniversary of the Hungarian Revolution of 1848. For this once-in-a-century celebration Imre was the keynote speaker. He found out about his imminent fatherhood too late and couldn't get home to Judit until the next day. The distance was only seven kilometers, yet a world apart without a telephone connection. How proud he was that his first child was born on that day—an ultimate symbol of patriotism! At the same time he felt awfully embarrassed that the holiday had prevented him from being at Judit's side, especially after he learned about the precarious delivery. As was customary in the village, Judit delivered not in a hospital but at home with the help of a local midwife. When a complication occurred, a massive bleeding, no doctor was available. It was the midwife's ingenuity that saved Judit's life; she sat on Judit's belly, which compressed her aorta.

When the remorseful Imre finally arrived home, there was barely any life in her. Consumed with worry over her wife, he failed to experience the rapture which he expected to feel for his firstborn. Judit sensed that and it pained her.

Like loving mothers the women of the parish cared for Judit and their yet unnamed daughter. The mother's name was an obvious choice for the child, except the baby didn't look like a "Judit." Imre blurted out the word Zizi. The name stuck, and now she was theirs. Very small in size, she looked more like a Zizi, whatever that meant.

Zizi was anything but a picture baby. Nobody praised the child. Imre never seemed to notice; the first awkward smile from this new little creature captured his being. Their old neighbor who began to take care of Zizi, apologized weeks later for not being more polite, but argued, "There was simply nothing to be praised in that child." That brought laughter, which freed the parents from their anxiety about their tiny offspring.

Their blessed state of parenthood was short-lived. Judit's stepmother appeared on the scene and announced her claim on their child as her rightful reward for taking in the orphaned Judit. They were shocked and outraged, as any parent would be, over such absurdity. Their little Zizi was only six months old! How could this woman, who had displayed such bizarre, personality-disordered behavior in raising Judit, presume to possess the skills to care properly for an infant? But the stepmother had her ways of blackmailing Imre and overpowering Judit. The young parents felt disarmed and helpless as their child was taken away. Their only comfort was the short distance between their homes and the fact that Zizi's grandfather was a kind and loving gentleman.

With their loss Judit and Imre grappled with very different guilt. Her guilt stemmed from her weakness, for not resisting. She even had to express gratitude toward her abuser. Even more upsetting was the realization that she could live without her child. Oddly enough, Imre too was the victim of his own gratitude, for his mother-in-law had given him Judit in marriage. She could silence Imre with a single look.

Judit and Imre struggled to recover from their humiliation. They were decent parents, yet they gave up their little girl they adored because they were incapable of standing up to a tyrant. Surely, their "child of the revolution" could have expected a greater measure of rebellion from her parents.

CHAPTER 4

Idealism at Work

I mre had been a Marxist theoretician and a member of the Romanian Communist Party from its inception. As Marxist ideals began to distort into Stalinist totalitarianism after 1949, his party comrades suddenly remembered Imre's earlier defiance and declared him "unworthy of the trust of the Communist Party" because of his ministry which now classified him as "reactionary clergy." Not only was he expelled from the Party, but he lost his teaching position in the college. Judit was also fired from her state job, as were all other wives of clergy all over the country. The passion to teach, however, could not be so easily taken away from them. The congregation of Siménfalva was a perfect community in which to put their idealism to work, to raise the cultural, spiritual and economic level of their people. In this village Imre wanted to build God's kingdom.

The parish's only classroom, which they called *Szeretet Otthon* [Home of Love], became a welcoming place for serious learning. Imre boldly dismissed the Communist Party's insistence on limiting the religious education of children to one hour per week. In Siménfalva each age group had classes twice a week. Imre wrote and home-published a new curriculum for religious education. His stories fascinated children and adults alike.

The evenings were reserved for adult education. Issues regarding youth ranged from hygiene, etiquette, socializing, dancing and courtship, to respect for their parents and their cultural heritage. Counseling young couples and parents and consulting with farmers about economic proficiency and modern agriculture involved the entire village. Imre began building a library by purchasing the literary classics and contemporary masterpieces for both adults and children. Book packages arrived monthly and people flocked to the parsonage for book loans. To their great pleasure people began to form a habit of reading serious literature. During long winter nights they had book discussions in the parsonage, where the women brought their needlework and spinning—all by the light of oil lamps, for the village didn't have electricity.

Central to their educational goals was preparing high school graduates for university admission. Siménfalva excelled in the number of university students. Six talented young men chose the Unitarian Seminary during Imre's twelve years of ministry. They told Imre that they had been inspired by him.

Siménfalva became one great family in an unprecedented sense. The large Gypsy population was welcomed by the Unitarian church, and that was unusual for that period. Their craft of basket weaving enabled more and more families to afford houses in the heart of the village instead of the outskirts.

Until 1959 Imre held the prestigious office of regional President of the League for Peace. His famous speech in which he drew a parallel between Marxist and Christian ideals was broadcast by the national radio. It was clear that party officials were using him to popularize the new communist ideology; but he was pursuing his own mission, to responsibly prepare his people for the coming ideological changes.

Forced collectivization was the first disaster of the new Communist era. Parishioners turned to the minister with their agonizing dilemma: should they give in to pressure and give up the land of their ancestors and the livelihood of their families, or resist and face the dangerous political consequences of arrest and imprisonment? The Communist witch hunt, the grand theater of an evil empire with its show trials and deportations, had already begun in the late 1940's. The Danube Canal constructions had already claimed its first victims. Fear began to creep into people's lives, like slowly acting poison. Siménfalva was not immune to the demoralizing effect of fear. The violent pressure, the daily intimidation campaign to force people to sign the agreement of entering the *collective* and thus voluntarily becoming destitute, broke the backbone of the village and of the church. Losing patience, the Communists went on a rampage and officially declared small landowners and well-equipped farmers to be *kuláks*, which was the equivalent of being an "enemy of the people." The state now had the right to confiscate all the property of these "reactionary" families. With such intimidation tactics, the rest of the community, family after family, signed the "membership application." Strong men of the proud and free Székely people, who for centuries had withstood invasions by Tartars and Turks in defense of the Eastern borders of Europe, were weeping in shame and helplessness.

With all their heart, Imre and Judit tried to raise the spirits of their parishioners. In the beginning he encouraged them to resist the pressure, but later he supported them in whatever decision they might have taken to protect their families and their freedom. Compromise was unavoidable at that point. As the secret police seized more and more people, Imre had to come to terms with the painful reality that some of his parishioners could turn into Communist collaborators. This was, after all, the ultimate goal of the Securitate. In his heart, however, he could never imagine anybody turning into a Judas. They were his people. He knew them! His trust of each member of his village was unconditional and unbroken. In the midst of the unrelenting political pressure, he thought that they grew even closer to each other. Imre tried to be their good shepherd and nurture their hope.

The church had a central role in the life of the village, and the minister was the most respected leader of the community. When the need arose for community volunteering, it was the minister's job to invite his parishioners. If the minister asked them for even an entire day of work, they did not hesitate to do so. On his bicycle, a rare luxury at that time, Imre made a round each evening to assign the next day's volunteers for an ongoing project. In this way they were able to build the village's cultural center, a large multifunctional building, in just a few months. This modern facility was long overdue and it was their first community project, a great success. They held balls, harvest festivals, choir singing, poetry recital and drama contests. Their theater and folk dance performances attracted people from the entire valley. Judit found her niche as a director of an amateur theater troupe and a trainer for the village's dance group. She put her medical interest to work too, training women in first aid and nursing, and they won several regional contests.

The ministerial couple were expected to be present in all aspects of life, even at the soccer games. The congregation would follow its minister from church service to the soccer field. They also opened the evening dance parties at their only pub's backyard on warm summer evenings. The intelligentsia of the village—the teachers, the Party secretary, the shopkeeper, the doctor, and the minister—constituted their own coherent community. They socialized together regularly at various functions, from dinner parties and dances at the local pub, to hiking trips and picnics.

Their lives were full of joy. The pinnacle of it was the birth of their son Andor on October 3, 1952. He was a most handsome baby. Zizi called him *Jesus*.

Academia and Politics, Victories and Tribulations

Shortly after he had settled in Siménfalva and had started his graduate studies toward a master's degree in Practical Theology, Imre proposed the ambitious project of writing a comprehensive intellectual history of Unitarianism as reflected in four centuries of sermonic literature. As it turned out, he actually conceived of a new discipline within Practical Theology. He planned to accomplish it in two steps. The sixteenth through the eighteenth centuries would be his master's thesis, and the nineteenth, "the great Unitarian century," his doctoral dissertation. The two main Unitarian libraries of Transylvania, the Great College Library and Archive in Kolozsvár, which contained the world's largest collection of Renaissance and Radical Reformation material, and the *Teleki Téka* in Marosvásárhely, offered á wealth of primary sources for his research. He also appealed to the Unitarian clergy to assess the surviving sermons in their parish archives, but was told that the two world wars had sadly caused their irreparable destruction.

Siménfalva was far away from both libraries, so for years Imre divided his time between his parish and Kolozsvár. He buried himself in the fascinating world of the Unitarian past in order to reenvision its future. As it turned out, no scholar before him had read through the thousands of mostly handwritten and frequently Latin sermons of four hundred years. Imre's training in paleography and Latin served him well here. He followed the leading thread of the evolving Unitarian thoughts through changing times and style—often hidden in coded language because of various persecutions. His thesis was highly praised by professors of the Protestant Theological Institute, and he received his master's degree *summa cum laude* on October 30, 1956.

The awarding ceremony coincided with the glorious high point of the Hungarian Revolution, just across the border. For many years Imre and his parishioners secretly listened to Radio Free Europe and Voice of America, the two Western stations aimed at Eastern block countries— forbidden fruits, except for the brave. They wanted to hear the voice about freedom. "Hold on! Resist Communism! You are not alone! We of the West are ready to help you! Revolt!" Hungarians did and they were victorious. The borders seemed to become transparent during those days when people of Hungary and Hungarians in Transylvanian celebrated their victory over Communism.

When the Soviet tanks raided the streets of Budapest on November 4, 1956, and Hungarian Prime Minister Imre Nagy broadcasted the heartbreaking last cry for help from behind the barricades, "Help us, help us! Help!" the President of the United States did not hear it nor did he send help. The Soviets filled the streets of Budapest with gallows and corpses. Students and even children carried on their violent resistance with Molotov cocktails against Soviet tanks, but the massacre continued. No help arrived. The West had betrayed Hungary. Yet the people of Transylvania continued to hold on to their hope that American and British liberators would eventually come to their help. "They'll come, they promised," Imre insisted. In the meantime more and more people disappeared from their homes. All his parishioners except one stopped coming to the parsonage to listen to the radio broadcasts. They apologized. "I am afraid. I am not strong enough to withstand interrogation. My family could suffer. Please understand me." Listening to Western broadcasts qualified as treason.

　　With all the grief over the cataclysm in Hungary, the scholar in Imre experienced a great sense of urgency. He set his sights on a faculty position in Practical Theology at the Seminary at Kolozsvár, and without delay he enrolled in the doctoral program as its only Unitarian candidate at that time. He intensified his work, adding to it the research of the homiletical and liturgical services of the Unitarian Church in the nineteenth century. It was a most rewarding project because of the wealth of primary sources from this time. Radical changes in theology and in the social involvement of the Transylvanian church in its embrace of the European Enlightenment, had greatly enriched the sermonic fruit. Imre always believed that the pulpit had been central to social changes, and needed to be, as both a reflecting and an inspiring forum. The literature of the pulpit during the Enlightenment reinforced his intuition. To discover the entire Unitarian spiritual-intellectual heritage, barely known and rarely touched, was worth living for.

　　Luckily, the Unitarian College Library was still in the possession of the Church, so Imre had unlimited access to all of its materials. He finished his doctoral program and wrote his dissertation within three years. The chair of the doctoral committee Prof. Dániel Borbáth, and the Rector of the school Prof. Gyula Dávid considered his work to be a unique contribution to historiography and predicted a great scholarly future for him. Imre was a step away from his ultimate professional goal, a faculty position at the Theology School where he could train future generations of ministers. A sudden vacancy in the Practical Theology chair was a thrilling surprise. Despite everything going on, things looked good for the GellÈrd family.

　　The doctoral award ceremony was scheduled for the end of November, 1959. Back in Siménfalva a celebration awaited the end of long years of sacrifices. It had been most unusual for a full-time village pastor to accomplish scholarship of this breadth. Judit awaited a more stable life. She deserved immeasurable credit for carrying on during his absence.

Her unconditional support of her husband at the price of her own career, her energetic community leadership, and her role as a model wife and mother were undoubtedly crucial to Imre's success.

In those days Imre filled every scrap paper with his new signature, with the "Dr." in front! There was such power in those two letters! That power was almost his. Almost. Such power was considered too dangerous to be bestowed upon Imre Gellérd.

* * *

The turbulent Unitarian Synod of 1946 had elected Dr. Elek Kiss as the twenty-seventh Bishop of the Unitarian Church. The rival candidate Dr. Dániel Simén, Imre's adored mentor, lost the race and felt vanquished. His wounded pride would affect the Gellérd family's life much deeper than Imre could have anticipated. Simén turned Imre into his trophy and comforter. He not only demanded Imre's exclusive loyalty, but he did so against the Bishop. Imre considered his costly friendship to be an ultimate honor, a view which Judit did not share. She was very critical of Dr. Simén because, she argued, he "enslaved" Imre and openly harmed his career. Judit and Imre rarely quarreled—he typically shrank back from open confrontation—but they had some dramatic clashes around the Simén's. Judit was jealous of them, and they were jealous of Judit, Imre thought. The tension between Judit and the Simén's exploded when the first congregation of Kolozsvár unexpectedly invited Imre to become their minister. Judit was jubilant, but Simén vehemently opposed it. "The parsonage at Kolozsvár was unhealthy and the salary too small for a decent living," he argued. "You have a little kingdom in Siménfalva, a large, elegant parsonage with gardens, orchids, and farmlands. Why would you give them up?" Of course, Dr. Simén was arguing for what was best for himself, not Imre. He and his wife Aranka loved to spend their summer vacation at the parsonage in Siménfalva. They enjoyed Judit's excellent cooking, and he took pride in becoming Zizi's godfather. Dr. Simén paid a short, surprise visit to Siménfalva to make sure Imre would not accept the invitation. Needless to say, Simén left the village victoriously; Imre gave up on moving to Kolozsvár.

At that time Judit suffered from Basedow disease, which caused extreme anxiety and emotional outbursts. The disease developed into a life-threatening *thyreotoxicosis* and she needed immediate thyroid surgery. It was during those weeks of Judit's hospitalization that Imre fully appreciated his wife's role in carrying the burden of their large household and the twenty or so house guests per week. It took Imre's sister and a host of other women to attempt to live up to Judit's lavish hospitality when the Simén family arrived for their usual weeks-long summer vacation. With Judit in the hospital in critical condition and with the needs of their children and the vacationing Simén's constantly requiring attention, Imre had a hard time focusing on Simén's ambitious projects that required more writings from Imre. His chronic insomnia became convenient, for he was left alone in the wee hours of the night to write for Simén's ongoing project, the in-house publication of brochures of Unitarian sermons. This series of sermons were to be appendices to Simén's Homiletics course and would serve as educational material for seminary students and sources of inspiration for ministers.

In the summer of 1958 the deputy Bishop of Hungary Rev. István Pethö visited Transylvania and came across Simén's publications. He enthusiastically took a few copies of the sermon collection with him back to Budapest. At the border Romanian guards searched him, found the brochures and confiscated them. So many things were seized at that border from so many people that this incident could have passed as unimportant. But it turned into a nightmare for those who happened to be authors in these publications. The copies fell into the hands of the Securitate, and among those authors were the best, the "most wanted," in the Church. The Securitate's "ear-on-duty" at the Church linked the authors to the incriminating literature and then played the role of the formal "denouncer," a necessary condition for political arrest.

In April, 1959, Dr. Simén was arrested, the first in this group of authors. He was the licensed publisher of the Homiletics course, but he lacked an official permit for the publication of the appendices. Next to be arrested was István Kelemen, who happened to stencil copy Simén's brochures. Kelemen was the new General Secretary of the Unified Protestant Theological Institute, which had just formed when, at state order, the Calvinist (*Református*), Lutheran and Unitarian seminaries were "integrated," effectively ceasing the independent status of the Unitarian seminary. Vilmos Izsák instantly seized Kelemen's job. He would turn the Theological Institute into a breeding ground for the recruitment of seminarians and ministers for Securitate collaboration and more.

Imre's fear grew into panic. Who would be next and when? It seemed to be only a matter of time before he would be arrested too.

CHAPTER 5

The Black Jeep

November 5, 1959, was a fairly typical day. Judit had invited some friends over for dinner in a customary celebration of Imre's patron saint's day. As usual she dazzled the guests with her culinary creations. As bubbly as a fine champagne, she didn't notice Imre's extreme anxiety.

Earlier that day Imre had been confidentially told that he would be arrested that night. Their trusted parishioner, with whom Imre had listened to Radio Free Europe and who had remained faithful to the end, had betrayed him, yet was generous enough to warn him of the impending danger. Those few hours of sheer agony were also a blessing for Imre, for he had time to hide the only copies of his four precious manuscripts: his master's thesis, his doctoral dissertation and his two novels. One novel was a historical novel about a controversial Unitarian figure Prince Mózes Székely, a native of Siménfalva, and the other a sort of autobiography written for children.

Although Imre was frantic, the concern for the security of his treasures took precedence over fear for his own life. It was now that he realized with dismay the depth of his community's demoralization: he did not dare to trust anybody with these treasures. He questioned his closest friends' trustworthiness. Moreover, he feared that he might harm someone by exposing the person to the danger of hiding his writings. Anybody could break under the pressure tactics of the Securitate. He finally took his writings to the attic of the parsonage. He tore open the floor boards of the attic and hid his spiritual children in their graves. He carefully nailed the boards back into place. Would he ever see them again, or would someone else find them? The Securitate? Perhaps his children, long after his death?

Imre Gellérd was thirty-nine years old, a servant of God, father of two young children, a husband deeply in love with his beautiful wife, and a minister to a devoted village that he had nurtured for twelve years. He was at the threshold of becoming *Dr.* Imre Gellérd, that "somebody" he had dreamed into being.

He tried to hide his panic, but was unable to cope with it alone. His best friends, some teachers next door with whom he shared his affliction, begged him to flee, to hide–to do something to avoid arrest. Yet they all knew too well how absurd any attempt of escape would be. So Imre went home and helped the unsuspecting Judit prepare dinner.

41

That night every word and every gesture became pregnant with new meaning. He saw everybody and everything in a glowing newness, as if for the first time, and for the last time. He desperately wanted to imprint the face and laughter of Judit into his mind forever. He wanted to remember the sweet touch of his seven-year-old son Andor. He wished he could say good-bye to Zizi who was far away studying at a music conservatory, so he wrote her a hurried letter.

Imre did not feel like going to sleep after the guests had left. He wished to prolong this last hour of bliss with his wife, who was so happy, so vivacious! He now realized that he had never watched her undress. How beautiful her breasts and her thighs, how radiant her whole being was. Oh, he wanted this moment of intimacy to last for eternity. Now she was leaning against the warm ceramic stove, relaxed, in a transparent nightgown, naked underneath, so angelic, so painfully beautiful! She brought in a glass of their homemade cherry wine the guests loved so much, and they drank from a shared cup. She had another surprise—an orange, the rarest delicacy. She peeled it and fed it to Imre. He needed it more, she argued, because of his chronic hepatitis. The last tests had been alarming; his illness could turn toward fatal cirrhosis. Their best friend has died of it at a young age a few years ago. Oh, what good care she had taken of him all these years. And he had always been so busy with his ministry, and research, and writing. Oh, to think what could have been! Now that he had completed his degree program, they would spend more time together. They would hike, even travel to see the countryside. Soon he would be a professor and they move to Kolozsvár, the place of their dreams. Judit would love the opera, the theater, and the fine social life. Oh, how guilty he felt for her loneliness and overworked life, for not being a good husband to her. He loved her more than anyone, more than his own life, but somehow they had never had enough time for each other.

She now revealed something so strange, she was scared. Last night in her dream the ceramic stove, the hearth in their bedroom, had broken diagonally into two pieces, as if lightening had hit it. One half shattered, then half of her wedding ring suddenly turned black as charcoal.

"Oh, Judit, Judit," Imre moaned inwardly. "You have no idea who is approaching our home, this perfect paradise. Oh, God, perhaps we see each other for the last time! I need more time. Give me more time, just a little more time to tell her, to show her how much I loved her! How can I leave my son, my joy Andor, sleeping sweetly? Look at him! Barely seven, he needs me. I am in charge. You trusted him with me. I must graft roses into his soul. I am the best teacher, and my son is my most sacred task. Please give me time, Lord! You are Perfection but there is a fatal mistake under way! You cannot, you must not take away my chance to say good-bye to the bright star of my life, Zizi."

Judit finally blew out the oil lamp. The village sank into heavy dreams and tormenting nightmares. But sleep would not visit Imre that night.

The black jeep of the Securitate had long since arrived and was waiting in the dark street in front of the parsonage. This was the most feared moment; people disappeared from their homes overnight, always at night. Black jeeps appeared and the next morning a family was devastated. Fathers, husbands and sons, wives and mothers were kidnapped. Some never came back.

In an instant a dozen bright flashlights burst through the always unlocked door of the parsonage. Pitch darkness was now juxtaposed with blinding, brilliant light, as if evil and good met. Judit had just gone to sleep. Imre was lying there, waiting for his inevitable hour of agony, surrendering to the darkness. He kissed his wife gently. The small army of Securitate officers crowded into the room, surrounding their bed. There seemed to be about seven of them. Panic-stricken by the surrealistic scene, Judit began to cry. They were ordered to light the oil lamp and put on clothes. One of the officers showed Imre a warrant for the house search. He had long expected and feared it. Few in those years escaped a house search, one of the overtures of prosecution.

Shivering from the cold and fear Judit was asked to leave the house and escort a few officers to the barns, the cellar, the attic, even into the well. Imre tried to keep an eye on her through the window. The officers searched and ravaged everything. Books were thrown off the shelves, beds and wardrobes turned upside down, paintings taken off the walls. It felt like an earthquake that shook their sensibilities and their lives irreversibly. The most wrenching of all was watching his handwritten sermons and manuscripts rummaged and scattered as the officers stepped on them with their muddy boots in callous disregard. Those dearly begotten writings, carved from the sweat of his brow, carried his very soul within their lines. He knew now the humiliation that rape victims knew.

A slim hope flashed through his mind. Given the lack of incriminating "evidence," perhaps the arrest would not occur? The officers reconvened in the bedroom. In an awkward but typical display of hospitality, Judit offered them cookies and wine. *These* guests, however, quickly rejected her magnanimity. There was a heavy, pregnant silence. Finally the feared moment arrived. One of the officers stepped forward and presented Imre with the warrant for his arrest. The room began to whirl around him. His head throbbed with an exploding headache. Judit was ordered to pack him food for three days, a couple changes of underwear and a warm outfit. Paralyzed by the shock, she obeyed like a robot.

The officers tried to trivialize the drama. The Rev. Gellérd, they told Judit, needed to clarify certain "misunderstandings," that's all. He would be home in no time. How much they wanted to believe it! Hope can be so irrational at times. They both knew there was no precedence for so happy an outcome.

The point in time of their inevitable separation arrived. Imre kissed his little son, who woke up just for a fleeting smile and an unsuspecting good-night. Then he held Judit with his whole being, keeping the moment captive for eternity. As Imre stepped out of their home, surrounded by the armed hounds, he continued to look back at Judit, trying to engrave her face, now distorted by pain, into his heart forever. Just before he reached the jeep, Judit began to run after them in desperation, crying with a loud voice. Suddenly she fell on the cement walkway and didn't get up. Was she knocked unconscious? Imre could not take this. He jerked his arms out from the grip of the officers and started to run back to Judit. But an iron clasp snatched him and pushed him into the back seat of the Jeep.

He was immediately blindfolded and they rode away. He sat in the suffocating grip of the officers. Now they became rude and abusive. Imre tried to keep his sense of direction and to guess where they were heading. They must have left the village when the Jeep stopped. Imre was pulled out of the vehicle and pushed against the parapet of a bridge. He recognized the place by hearing the sweet gurgle of the Nyikó creek underneath. He used to rest at this bridge every time he walked between the village and the college. It was a favorite spot for children and youth, a cool getaway on Sunday afternoons.

Suddenly a horrifying prospect drained all his strength. He could be shot at the spot! People disappeared all the time and no one knew whether they were dead or alive. Yes, he concluded, this must be the firing squad which would execute him at the edge of his own village. His entire life elapsed into this last moment. Time becomes vertical before the moment of death. Imre felt a strange inner peace as he visualized his loved ones and listened to the morning bell of his church ringing its celestial farewell. "Here I am, Lord!" he whispered.

The officers' insults and diabolical laughter seemed like distant echoes of a surrealistic present. One of them slapped his face, another kicked his legs. He grabbed at the bridge and barely kept his balance, hanging onto the railing for dear life. One of them sneered, "Look back now, if you can see through the blindfold, for you won't see your damn church again!" He was squeezed back into the gut of the Jeep.

It was dawn by the time they arrived at the Securitate in Székelykeresztúr, Imre's beloved college town. He was locked up in the basement of a building which was just one block away from the home of Judit's parents. The interrogations began instantly. They were but an innocent foreplay of what the next five months would bring.

Back in Siménfalva no one opened the door of the parsonage on the day of Imre's arrest. If people had once thought they would die for the minister they loved so much, now any intention to reach out with help to his family was checked by the pervasive fear. That was the beginning of their demoralization.

At noon the Securitate's black jeep stopped again in front of Imre's parsonage. They had come back for Judit. They loaded her in and whisked her away. This time, though, a group of women rushed into the parsonage to make sure her son was okay. Before they could work out a plan for his care, Judit was released and returned safely.

Secret Police Face to Face

After three days Imre was transferred to the dreaded Securitate prison in Kolozsvár. It was known as the "academy" for the application of the most sophisticated methods of torture. The Romanian Securitate had learned and then perfected the Soviet and North Korean brainwashing techniques. Imre had heard rumors about this infamous place. Now he had the "opportunity" to experience it firsthand.

At the beginning he was assured that the whole procedure would be "just a little clarification of some misunderstandings." His innocence was obvious, they assured him, so he shouldn't worry. Of course, the length of the investigation would depend on the level of his cooperation. They locked him up for three days in a two-meter by two-meter underground cell with no window, to grant him peace for undisturbed reflections. His migraine headaches, exacerbated by the lack of medicine, consumed most of his energy.

When they moved him into a larger dormitory his situation worsened. He could not sleep. All night long the prisoners were forced to sleep on their backs with their arms on the covers and an unbearable bright light in their faces. The room had four iron bunk beds, and each bed accommodated two or three people. Only whispering was allowed. There was no *kübli* [bucket or slop pail] and they were left to the mercy of the guards to take them to the bathroom, blindfolded. They hurried them, never allowing them enough time. At the beginning some of his peers refused the hogwash-like food, but soon hunger forced them to eat anything they were given.

The place was sheer hell, not because of physical tortures but rather the psychological warfare against them. When the cell door opened, they automatically jumped. Detainees had to face the walls and never dare to look back until permission was given. At any unusual noise they panicked—it might be the next interrogation. Earsplitting screams of those under torture insured the continuous presence of fear. For several days at a time interrogations were conducted day and night, so intensely that the subject would collapse in exhaustion from the fear, stress and sleep deprivation. The prisoners knew that it could happen to anyone, at any time, even in the middle of the night. It could last for a few hours or a few days. Then for weeks nothing happened. But the intense waiting in a high alert mode, all the time, slowly altered their state of consciousness.

Sleep deprivation, added to fear, produced short episodes of psychosis in some of the detainees. After only a few days in this state of "de-realization," some gave in, admitting the false charges against them just to avoid more torture. This typically happened after exposures to crushing interrogation sessions, in which the victim was promised a much worse one in two weeks. Some simply could not bear the uncertainty and volunteered to tell "everything," far beyond the truth or what was expected. In their distorted sense of reality, they often recited what they already knew was expected from them. Many had no idea what the reason was for their arrest in the first place.

Rumors circulated that detainees were being doped through their food, and the rumors turned out to be true. The drugs resulted in weakening their will power, causing the state of *abulia*. Crushing their volitional strength, thereby increasing their suggestibility for mental and verbal manipulation, was a precondition for brainwashing.

In Imre's case the doping was massive. Some kind of psychotropic drug was administered to him through regular injections. The result was that he became increasingly disoriented and his overall memory and self-awareness failed. He realized with horror his deepening amnesia for everything in his "previous" life in the outside world. In his clearer moments he recognized that he had been under a training regimen to memorize his "part" in his own trial. He was being coerced to rehearse his confessional role as a defendant and his witness role against his colleagues and friends at their group trial. This was not all. The more alarming effect of the doping on all the detainees was a compulsion toward self-accusation, built upon their weakened will power and fear. Imre's desire to see his family was so tormenting that he was often tempted to volunteer to confess anything that might buy his way out from that hell. Yet he consciously tried to hang onto his sanity. He tried to split his own personality so that the psychologist in him would observe the process of deterioration in his psyche and generate enough will power to resist it.

Imre's worst fear was not from death but from the possibility of failing to withstand the torture and inadvertently becoming a secret police informer. He was physically weak, he was tormented by daily migraine headaches, and he was innately timid. With his remaining mental powers he tried to stay focused on resisting the coercion to sign the document of denouncement. This was a list of some twenty names, mostly unknown to him, but among them his best friend, the Rev. Áron Török, a brilliant student of his and a Unitarian minister-poet. He had shared Imre's last hours of freedom at that last supper at home, and now Imre's task was to incriminate him, to become his formal "denouncer." In those show trials nothing was left to chance; everything was orchestrated with great sophistry.

The Securitate teams worked in turns and alternated their techniques of torture. Some were brutal and abusive, physically and especially emotionally. They mocked and humiliated the prisoners over and over, beyond what they thought they could endure. Then another team took over, exhibiting kindness and compassion. They tried to pose as friends who were protecting their interests. Sweet promises of release, visits with family members, and other favors were offered. "Why is it so big a deal to sign this document in exchange for your immediate release and rejoining your family? Rev. Török will be arrested no matter what. We can do it without your signature; we will simply find someone else to sign. It is just a matter of time. But then you will lose your once-in-a-lifetime chance. You are stupid enough to turn yourself into a sacrificial lamb for nothing!" So argued the "good" officer. The dilemma and temptation and guilt tore at Imre. It took an iron will to resist the promise of freedom. He feared this tactic more than the brute physical punishment. The longing for his family was an all-consuming fire in him. "What if I just signed this damned paper? If I don't, someone else will. But then it won't be I who gets the reward." His best defense was trying to keep the principle in mind. "Only the principle mattered! The bottom line was, I had to keep my integrity. I must not harm others, no matter what the price. I must not sell my soul to this evil."

As vulnerable and timid as he initially felt, the occasional realization that the Securitate underestimated his strength exhilarated him. Then came the next injection to blur his mind again, and when it cleared up, he was terrified once more, for he did not remember what he had said or done while under the drug's effect. The fear of himself, of his possible weakness, terrified him more than the interrogations. "I was losing my mind, I feared. But when the officer presented the same list again, I felt a strange relief. I did it! I mean, I didn't do it! I was able to resist them. I am strong, after all. God is with me. And I prayed to God ever more fervently to strengthen my resolve, to shield my core humanity in this madness, and to give thanks for this victory." That keen focus to which he was attuned— not to harm others, not to become a betrayer and a secret police informer— grew in him like a beacon in the bleakness. His conscience, that small but most relevant part of his brain, was""on duty" always, to resist, to reject temptations and to save his integrity even when pain and fear and drugs were dehumanizing the rest of his being.

During this quest for coerced confessions, one was never sure that a misinterpreted word would not be used toward someone's arrest, perhaps one's best friend. The secret police's final objectives were to destroy their prisoners' dignity, to coerce them to compromise their moral integrity. Resistance required strength of conscience, which not all had. To those who might have broken down under such circumstances, there should be no condemnation.

"I was not a brave man; I had been weak and depressed. But I managed to escape the self-humiliation of becoming a Judas. I managed to stay clean. Although I believed then that I could have negotiated my freedom and escaped from this prison hell, I could not betray my principles. My integrity is more important to me than freedom or happiness. What I did was not heroism; it was the only right thing to do. I felt terrible about my family, for whom I was responsible. On the other hand, I couldn't have faced my children, I couldn't have lived if I had betrayed my own humanity."

Where is My Father?

Zizi was eleven years old during that time. It was Christmas vacation and she had just arrived in Siménfalva after a long semester at a school far away.

"My daughter will study to become a Gypsy," her father had teased her proudly. With her violin in hand Zizi had left for boarding school in the prestigious music and art school of Marosvásárhely. Once there, it seemed nobody cared about her any more. Her mother paid her a brief visit once, but she hadn't seen her father for three months. His only letter to her made her cry for days. "I had been always hungry and cold in my childhood; now I work for my precious daughter to have a happier childhood," he had written. Well, Zizi was already quite happy, a straight A student, and studying violin with a famous Jewish violin teacher Editha Mátyás-Broch. But all the love she received from her teachers could not alleviate the longing she felt for her parents.

Finally, on this Christmas Eve the bus roared through the last turn to their village. At the bridge she glimpsed the steeple of the Unitarian church. Her heart leaped into her throat. What a perfect time to come home for her first vacation! She and her dad would go "angel watching" with her little brother, who still believed in the angel story. She was home at last!

Zizi's mother and brother were waiting for her at the bus stop. "Where is Father?" she asked. Zizi stared at her mother, shockingly thin and pale, and began to run toward the parsonage. Judit burst in tears. "Your father was arrested by the secret police two months ago. We don't know anything about him. We did not dare to tell you, to protect you from its consequences. This is why I did not dare to visit you. My heart was broken and yours would have been, too."

Christmas became a time of terrible grief for Judit and her children. At one point, after they had sung the traditional song "Angels From Heaven" under their Christmas tree, little Andor asked, "Why did God abandon us?"

The Grand Theater of an Evil Empire

The first open group trial by the Military Court of Kolozsvár was scheduled for April 8, 1960. These trials were later called "conceptual trials" because everything, including the sentence, was pre-conceived and prescripted. The trial itself was a mere enactment of the script, a play within the play.

Imre's trial was on May 18, 1960, seven months after his arrest. Except for the Rev. Áron Török all the other authors were arrested and tried. It was the day when he would finally see Judit, he hoped. As he was led into the courtroom, he gathered his energy to pull himself out of his mental haze. Sleep deprivation and doping the night before had drifted him into an altered state of consciousness. He was considered "ready" to testify, i.e., sufficiently brainwashed for the show trial. Despite his grogginess he realized that he might have fallen into some trap, but he had no comprehension of its nature.

He looked around the room, searching for Judit, and was shocked to see Dr. Simén. He hadn't seen his mentor for nearly a year. Then he finally glimpsed Judit. Her presence produced a bolt of happiness which jolted his sanity. Her face shined with joy while his convulsed with pain. Perhaps they were seeing each other for the last time. He wanted to carve her face into his memory forever.

Judit came to the trial with Ferenc, her husband's oldest brother, and Lajos Biró, a seminary students from Siménfalva. She had no doubt about Imre's innocence. Even the words used in the accusation, "enemy of the regime," sounded ridiculous. No incriminating material had been found in their home. Imre was the victim of his idol Dániel Simén, Judit concluded. Determined to clear her husband's name, she had sold everything she could and hired the best defense lawyer in that region. He had promised Judit her husband would be acquitted. "You will bring him home right after the trial," he had assured her. There was more reason for optimism after they discovered that the judge was Imre's former student. Hope suddenly had a shining face.

The military tribunal's courtroom was packed and hot. Judit held her breath in anxious anticipation of finally seeing her husband. The door opened and, sandwiched between two military officers, Imre entered the hall. Instead of wearing the prison uniform, he was dressed in his suit and tie—a good sign, the lawyer noted. Judit could barely hold back her tears. Her husband's face was pale and convulsed with suffering. As their eyes met she tried to convey her assurance and optimism. "Everything is all right. We will be going home together. Hold on! Be brave!" She gave him her best smile to fortify his frail figure.

The charges against Imre cited seven "reactionary" sermons which supposedly instigated against the social order and attempted to undermine

Communism's triumph. One sermon in particular dealt with the Kingdom of God at hand. "Aha! You mean America is your kingdom of God!" said the prosecutor. Imre thought they were joking. In another, a Christmas sermon, Imre had narrated the flight of Joseph, Mary and baby Jesus to Egypt to avoid Herod's massacre. "Aha! You mean that Herod is us and you hope that Egypt will be on the side of the imperialists!" If his life hadn't been in danger, Imre would have laughed out loud at such malignant ignorance.

Imre soon learned that all seven of his sermons had been used by Dr. Simén in those in-house publications. If they carried any revolutionary tone, it came from the hand-written corrections and insertions by Dr. Simén, who had edited and published the collection. One witness testified that the incriminating notes in the margins were in Dr. Simén's handwriting. Another witness testified that Dr. Simén had lacked an official permit for the publication of the sermons. The judge read the testimonies before the court and called Dr. Simén to answer the charges against him. Simén said, "I have never made any corrections and I never edited Imre Gellérd's manuscripts. All I did was correct his grammatical mistakes. I had no intention whatsoever to change their original content."

In a touching moment the judge rose to Imre's defense. "Don't you realize, Dr. Simén, how ridiculous and insulting your statement is? You and many others have lived by Imre Gellérd's intellectual brilliance, and you claim to be correcting his grammatical errors?"

In that moment of shock Imre was less concerned with the charges against him than the disturbing testimony by his beloved mentor. Dr. Simén had just refused to take responsibility for his own acts which would have diminished Imre's guilt, and incidentally, probably cleared Imre of the charges. He would have given his life for his idol, who now denied even his actual deeds. Imre thought it must be a mistake. He didn't remember rehearsing this part during his interrogations. It must be the effect of torture on Dr. Simén.

The atmosphere of the courtroom intimidated Judit, and she could barely follow the course of events. She trusted her lawyer, who seemed calm and optimistic throughout the short trial. It was finally Imre's turn to speak, to defend himself based on the right of "the last word." She smiled in anticipation of the words she was sure Imre would say to free himself from this place. Suddenly her face contorted in disbelief. Imre solemnly said, "Dr. Simén has denied making changes to my original texts, and I do not wish to contradict him. I take full responsibility for everything."

The defense lawyer turned to Judit in utter indignation. "Your husband has gone mad! He has just slammed the prison door on himself!"

"I couldn't bare it any longer," Judit remembered. "I saw my two children, waiting for their father to come home, yet here I saw that, for their father, Simén was more important than his own children. After first poisoning our marriage, that coward Simén has now sent his loyal disciple to jail. How could I ever forgive my husband for sacrificing his family for a vain idol who has just openly betrayed him? Has Imre truly lost his mind?"

With little to deliberate about, the judge read the verdict, Sentence #167 of the Military Court of Cluj: *"Imre Gellérd is hereby sentenced to seven years of prison and forced labor, with an additional five years of deprivation of his civil rights."*

There had been seven incriminating utterances, resulting in one year of prison each. The judge added that Dr. Simén would have received fourteen years, which would now be divided "fraternally" between the two of them. Justice had prevailed. Who could complain? *Finita est comedia!*

Imre was motioned to leave the courtroom. His mind numb he felt he might as well be dead. Ashamed to look at Judit directly, he glanced over just in time to see her collapse on the floor. People jumped to help her. She looked lifeless, crumpled in a heap. Had this ordeal killed her? "Please, let me...," he began, but the guard roughly pushed him through the door.

CHAPTER 6

The Art of Prison Living

Following the trial the Securitate transferred Imre, now a legitimate prisoner, to the feared prison in Szamosújvár [Gherla] on May 18, 1960, at age thirty-nine. Szamosújvár was one of the largest political prisons in Romania in the 1950's. Following the mass political arrests by the Gheroghiu-Dej government in 1959, nine thousand inmates were jammed into its three buildings. Prison cell #81, the "clergy's cell," was the largest, housing as many as a hundred prisoners in one big room. The dungeons of the prison's medieval buildings were infamous places for solitary confinement, the most dreaded form of punishment.

In 1958 the execution of ex-Prime Minister of Hungary Imre Nagy, a prominent leader of the Hungarian revolution in 1956, provoked a prison riot in Szamosújvár. Following the riot terror took over. Prison guards became deadly personal enemies of the inmates. Beatings and other cruel and humiliating punishments were frequent and unprovoked. The guards called out to them, *"Mai, banditule!"* [Hey, brigand or gangster!], a translation which only vaguely conveys the insulting tone of the Romanian original, especially when it was addressed to venerable bishops, professors, doctors, diplomats and writers.

Many of them survived, although not all. Some suffered terribly. Some could not endure it. Some lost their minds. Many died. It appeared that three factors were helpful to surviving: faith, a sense of humor, and assuming responsibility for the cause they believed in and which had led them to prison. Having at least one of these qualities or attitudes was essential for survival.

Faith in prison was not a mere theory or philosophy. Faith took on a form of affirmation: "My life is in the hands of God, who loves me. There must be some divine purpose in my suffering, but that knowledge is with God only. When the time comes, I will be set free. If not, God will take me to the beyond. My loved ones are also in God's care. My goal is to stay alive!" Those who were able to accept this simple hope were calm and radiated peace. They were able to help and encourage others, learn and teach, tell stories and listen to the stories of others. They were never bored and always busy. They lived.

A sense of humor was one's most precious quality. Their situation was so unbelievably grotesque that anybody with a minimal sense of humor couldn't help but see the ironical, humorous side of that life. Those who took the daily diabolical humiliations into themselves could not endure long and died. For many, humor turned things around. Once a new prisoner, a theologian, was instructed about house rules by the prison guard. After listening intently, the newcomer asked, "All right, but now tell me, what are we allowed to do?" Before the guard answered, the prisoner said, "I know! We can think." The guard, stupefied, yelled, "What? Think? Thinking is forbidden even outside of prison!" One had to laugh at this. Those who could, lived.

Assuming responsibility for their actions gave many of them tremendous strength. They said, "I had done something which I considered the right thing to do, and I would act in the same way today. I anticipated being arrested, but I faced the consequences of my actions. Now I must survive it." With this attitude one was able to take the blistering hatred of the guards with some immunity and stay invulnerable toward humiliation. One had to hold onto one's dignity and one's humanity. Those who did, lived.

While having any one of these three characteristics was enough to survive, those who had all three were able to create a lifestyle in prison. Physical strength was not a primary factor. It helped only the simpletons put up with prison life. Stupidity itself might actually have been an adequate factor for survival. Those who could not comprehend what was happening to them, who obeyed the guards' orders without experiencing the inherent humiliation, who gobbled down whatever swill was dished out–they too managed to live, but would one call this "life" even outside of prison?

The outside world was blocked to the prisoners, their isolation was so complete. Even the small windows were covered with wooden boxes, with only a tiny hole left which opened toward the sky. A young poet Ernö Számadó wrote these impressions:

> The rhythm of lines was taken away.
> Everything here is square, blocks and cubes.
> Iron crossbars frame even the sky,
> Dividing it into small eyes.

It would be a mistake to assume that the poets, writers, or other people in the prison were allowed or able to write. They were not, at least not on paper with pencil as we know it. Writers' expressions would be "written" into the memories of the inmates. Rev. László Varga, a Calvinist minister with an excellent memory, memorized many great poems as favors to his fellow inmates. This is one of them:

An Everyday Story[1]

The filthy dawn pours into
Our cell through blind windows.
The many shackles clank.
Wailing fills the prison.

One of us, a fellow prisoner is dying....
It is no big deal, he doesn't mind it either.
He is the next in the long line,
Of bodies, eroded by the'lead mine.

Prisons, beatings, chill and lead,
He slowly spat out his lungs.
"He will not live to see his home,"
Prisonmates whistle for him.

Like vultures, they watch him die,
then snap up his rummage,
and keep his death a secret
to have his last supper shared.

Nothing matters to him any more,
His eyes search the infinite.
Jesus, you might recognize him:
He is your brother, isn't he?

Did he ever have a mother?
Does a heart carry love for him?
Have mercy on her, for she is far,
And will not know that he is gone.

Tears will not fall
On his humiliated forehead,

After burning pain of longing,
Farewell is just more heartache.

The guards "summon him out."
No more shivering, no more hunger.
Dragging him down the stairs
His skull plays a funeral march.

On the cold stone of the dungeon
Rats dance a last ritual on his chest,
And by nightfall, the scribe
Erases his name from the list.

They suffered from many kinds of deprivations. Being deprived from reading and writing was as great a torment as hunger. During ward searches the discovery of the slightest trace of writing was cruelly punished. Yet the guards were never able to put an end to their resourceful, inventive ways of writing. They scraped the white wash of the wall with the soles of their boots. They wrote on pieces of torn bed sheets—a dangerous method, easily discoverable. The most advanced technology for secret writing was black laundry soap. Dried for two months and polished well on both sides, it served as a stone slate. Another material was bone, found occasionally in one's food, which also needed careful polishing. About the size of a man's palm, a slate could accommodate eighty words. That meant forty foreign words could be learned, or short essays written for learning grammar, or poems written to be learned by heart. Most of all, they were used for writing letters to loved ones, over and over again, on the same surface, erasing and starting once more.

Prisoners were often crushed with boredom and got into fights. Not in Cell #81, where almost all inmates were highly educated intellectuals. It was a prison college for them and might have been enjoyable if not for the miseries of forced labor, interrogations, solitary confinement and humiliations.

If they made it through the morning routine, in which a hundred prisoners jammed to get urgent access to the only toilet, then lined up for washing and lined again for a breakfast of black tea-like coffee and a slice of black bread, then their intellectual life could ensue. Depending on the

---

[1]"Mindennapi történet" by Ernö Számadó, memorized and reconstructed by László Varga in Hungarian, translated by Judit Gellérd.

inmates' daily programs and their interests, they gathered in groups and sat on someone's bed. Some groups encouraged participation in fascinating academic lectures, language teaching workshops, or heated political debates about how they would save the future of their nation. Other groups picked up the thread of a novel or story. Theologians held Bible courses and taught exegesis. Many great systems of thoughts were born in those cultured minds. Many ideas were tried out and polished in these discussions among the prisoners.

Imre usually taught psychology and philosophy, and his lecture series were very popular. They barely found enough room, using several neighboring bunk beds for the gatherings. Some in the audience with good memories were able to benefit from these lectures after prison. One of his friends, for example, built his post-prison doctoral dissertation on Imre's psychology lecture series. Learning about psychology surely helped many prisoners understand the brainwashing and humiliation that was inflicted upon them.

Many of the prisoners both learned and taught foreign languages. Imre taught French and learned English and German. Ironically, outside of prison studying English would have been dangerous, for it was considered the "American spy language." Here Imre was free to learn it.

Alongside his theology professor János Erdö, Imre focused his attention on the spiritually vulnerable younger prisoners. Many needed intense pastoral care because of two major dangers: lethargy or depression on the one hand, and excruciating sexual desire and food cravings on the other. The priests and ministers held regular theological-psychological discussions about these problems, trying to redirect destructive energies. Young intellectuals who were atheists suffered greatly. A Marxist student, sentenced to twenty-five years for a joke, and having already served six, refused to eat and starved himself to death. He was not alone in committing suicide in the prison.

Subtle Tortures

Intellectual preoccupation eased the prisoners' anguish, but that was not without risks. The worst kind of harm came from the inside informers who infiltrated the inmates' society. Usually they became wardsmen and had power over a hundred people. They could deny medical help in life-threatening emergencies. They could send their fellow prisoners to solitary confinement or inflict other suffering.

One "subtle" form of torture was the integration of mentally ill people. Schizophrenics whose delusions had political content were jailed instead of treated. Some were violent while others needed assistance to survive. Fortunately, there lots of inmates with plenty of time and good hearts. The situation was more tragic when prisoners lost their minds in prison. The first common symptom was gazing at the door and withdrawing from any social activity. These people's world shrank into one burning question: "Will I ever be free to see my family?" The existential quest grew into self-destructive delusions, clouding the person's mind.

Usually prisoners did not receive medical treatment in spite of living among medical doctors. There were two categories of doctors, the official prison physicians and the imprisoned physicians. The official ones were ex officio butchers. The imprisoned ones did what they could. One prisoner suffered from tuberculosis, but the official prison doctor denied him medication. The reason: in his file there was an instruction that he must not leave the prison alive. Fortunately, and illegally, an inmate doctor treated him with streptomycin. Groin mycosis became a form of torture for many. The itching and burning were unbearable. The prison doctors let the victims suffer for weeks and months. It was senseless suffering, worse than a beating, yet it was not even a "human rights issue."

There were periods when prisoners were forbidden to sit down for eighteen hours during the day. They were forced to stand or walk two or three steps in each direction because cells were overcrowded. If the guards caught any of them breaking a rule, the entire cell was punished. The guards would order them to drop down on their faces on the cold cement floor, or worse, to crawl under the beds and lie there for 20 to 30 minutes. Those who did not have room under a bed were stepped on and beaten by sadistic guards. The punishment for illegal napping could be solitary confinement in the dungeon with no blanket or mattress and barely any food for several days.

Most of the prisoners suffered from malnutrition and related diseases. Deliberate deprivation was an obvious tactic to weaken their resistance. The more people died in jail, the more""positive" the evaluation of the prison was. "We assure enough calories for you to breathe" was the slogan. Since the daily soup had lots of onion in it, prisoners requested that the onion be served to them raw rather than cooked. The guards' malicious reply to them was, "You have no right to vitamins!"

Dental problems were ignored entirely. Every once in a while an inmate dentist was ordered to pull out a prisoner's aching teeth without anesthesia and without verifying whether extraction was the proper treatment. Imre lost most of his teeth in five years.

Ordinary criminals such as murderers and thieves were segregated from the political prisoners, and they enjoyed greater privileges. For example, they were in charge of cooking and serving the meals for the political inmates, and they skimmed off the best food for themselves.

Prisoners were periodically transferred from one prison to another. The maximum time spent in one place was typically one year. By mixing the inmates every half year and assigning new and unknown inside informers, officials could control and discipline them better. These changes were somewhat beneficial for the inmates too, for after each of them had shared all his stories, life became boring and quarrels broke out more often. The quality of the company in a cell was essential for one's mental health.

Time Measured in Christmases

A certain social structure and hierarchy naturally evolved in any prison situation. The clergy enjoyed the highest status among prisoners. Roman Catholic and Greek Catholic bishops were imprisoned mainly because of their connection with Rome and because of their obstinacy to compromise. Their personal charisma and strong character earned them the highest respect. Franciscan monks and Protestant ministers in particular were kept in high regard because of their service and pastoral care to the prison community. Although rules strictly forbade religious activity, they found ways around those restrictions and at the risk of punishment held daily worship services in Hungarian and Romanian. These services were genuinely ecumenical. Extraordinary sermons were preached and prayers beseeched the heavens. In the midst of such misery, some inmates experienced moments of the sacred that taught more about humanity and faith than anything in free society could ever have.

They measured time without their families in Christmases and in languages they learned. Christmas was a special time that brought together Romanians, Hungarians, Saxons, Jews and atheists, creating a deep human bond among them that no church congregation would ever experience. The preparation for the Christmas service was an elaborate process. During the holy week they held penance and self-examination as a prerequisite for communion. Communion was desired by many, and they had to be creative in finding the elements. Throughout the year prisoners who officially suffered from malnutrition, that is, who had lost half their body weight,

were given *vinum ferri,* black current wine, because it was rich in iron.
The prison "protocol" required these inmates to share a thimbleful of it
with a priest or minister cell mate, who saved up the hidden booty until the
holidays.

When the much awaited day of Christmas arrived, they set the
"Lord's table" at the top of a four-story bunk bed, least visible from the
guards' peephole. A handkerchief was the ceremonial tablecloth. They .
diluted the precious wine with water in an aluminum mug. The breakfast
bread on Christmas morning served as communion bread, cut into tiny
pieces, one for each. The "congregation" simulated an ordinary discussion.
Some took turns in front of the door to interfere with the sight from the
guards.

On one memorable Christmas Rev. László Varga, a Calvinist pastor,
administered the communion. His hands trembled as he lifted the bread
and then the wine. "Take this...." In this primitive setting like that of the
early Christians, Jesus himself was among them that day, promising life
for them. Although said in stifled voices, their prayers were a glorious
exaltation. A golden chalice would never mean so much as that shabby
aluminum cup. An old Communist choked with sobs and they all followed.
For hours afterward nobody said a word. It was a sacred time of healing,
each facing the depth of his soul and being with his loved ones *in abstentia*
on Christmas.

The Romanian Gulag

In early fall of 1960 rumors started about a possible transfer of the
inmates from prison cells to labor camps, to the infamous Danube Canal.
They had mixed feelings about the news. On one hand, to be outside in the
fresh air, to see the sky and the trees again was an irresistible desire. On
the other, they knew too well that thousands of political prisoners had died
at the Danube during the previous reign of terror in the early 1950's.

In mid-October, 1960, a general appeal called upon the prisoners
to volunteer for the camps. When most cautiously declined, the appeal
turned into an order and those considered healthy were selected. Although
the official doctors examined the sick and malnourished, no one was found
unfit for forced labor.

Imre was selected for the second transport. At night officials loaded
a few hundred prisoners onto a special train made up of cattle cars disguised
as railway coaches. The windows were painted and sealed so no one could

look in or out. The air inside became thinner by the hour. The most "dangerous" inmates, those with more than a twenty-year sentence, were chained in small cages, six of them in one cubical. The rest traveled crammed together in larger cabins. The trip took many days, and nobody knew where they were heading. The only good thing in this ordeal was that they had regained possession of their luggage and thus were able to read from their hidden books and Bibles.

When the train crossed the Danube River, the first identifiable place on their itinerary, a sudden panic took over their cautious optimism. Were they being taken to the Soviet Union, to Siberia, or perhaps to the feared Gulag? In a few hours the cattle cars opened, fears evaporated, and they had their first illusion of freedom in almost two years of indoor confinement. The guards immediately herded them into a big cargo ship, and several hours later they docked at a no man's land in the Danube Delta. They were driven like animals out into the thick mud. Stupefied, they thought this would be their execution site. With the Danube at their back and an endless marsh around them, nobody would discover the killing of a few hundred prisoners there. Such scenarios were too well known from history. An armed unit surrounded them, pointing their weapons, as guards rounded up the prisoners like animals. Then began a long march in a sea of mud until they finally reached the labor camp of Salcea on the island in the Danube Delta. Salcea and Periprava were the large base camps, with extensions located in Grind and Gradina. The cold wind, the *Crivat,* blew ferociously. Most of them were so weak and exhausted that they had to gasp for air. Their worn boots stuck so deeply in the mud that each step took extreme effort. They were very hungry.

Upon their arrival the guards called for certain professionals— doctors, engineers, cooks, electricians—to step forward. Normally, any singling out was dangerous, but this time these lucky ones were appointed to enviable kitchen and maintenance jobs for the camp. The rest were locked up in barracks for days. Most of the clergy were soon transferred to other camps for reed cutting and corn harvesting.

Their labor camp was about four to five acres in size and surrounded by electric barbed wire and watchtowers. There was no way to escape from that place, not just because of the watchful eyes of armed soldiers but because the island was surrounded by dangerous marsh. There was no place to go. Even if someone escaped, Lipovan fishermen of the neighboring villages were bribed by the Securitate to capture any fugitive. Still, there were those who tried. When somebody did, rockets alarmed the entire camp in no time and the guards brought the fugitive back. The severe punishment seriously discouraged the rest of the prisoners from fleeing. Once, while they were working on the shore of the Danube, a young man jumped into the mighty river and disappeared in the dark. He was never found and one could only speculate whether he drowned or was shot, or perhaps he miraculously managed to swim to the other shore to the Soviet Union. Even if he had survived, a Soviet prison camp was his most likely destination. Despair, especially for those sentenced to life, was a strong and irrational driving force for taking chances.

The camp dormitory was one huge space in the bottom of a discarded French cargo ship stranded in the mire. Its once proud name *Liberté* became the epithet of the ship jail, even the symbol of their lives. During the winter the freighter with its metal walls would become an ice casket imbedded in the frozen Danube. During the hot summers the bowels of the ship would turn steaming and suffocating like a furnace.

About five hundred people were jammed into this space. Their bunk beds were built four stories high, and two or three inmates had to share one narrow bed, rendering impossible a restful sleep. The morning alarm thundered at 5 a.m. long before sunrise. Winter was approaching and they did not have adequate clothing. They received shabby, dirty uniforms and odd, worn-out boots left by previous prisoners. They collected pieces of rags and patched as many layers as they could onto their uniforms.

They suffered from hunger more in the cold. Breakfast consisted of watery soup made out of potato peel, spoiled cabbage and a few grains of barley, sometimes along with fake coffee and twelve grams of black bread. For lunch they got the only valued food *turtoi*, a piece of corn meal, with their swill-like soup. Dinner was more of the same. They barely ate any protein and almost never any dairy products. The daily forced march of six kilometers to their workplace and back was an additional strain to the eleven or twelve hours of labor. They left in the dark and arrived back in the dark. They were always unbearably hungry. They were always exhausted. Imre spent the next four years of his life here.

The first winter was especially harsh and cruel. The prisoners stayed captive in the unheated dormitory during winter storms but were not allowed to cover their feet with their blankets during the day. The punishment for those who broke this mad rule was fifty hits with a stick on their palms. One was considered lucky if his palms did not crack because then he wouldn't have been able to shovel and dig the next day, and that would bring about a whole avalanche of more punishments. Extremely bad weather actually meant relief for the prisoners. They were confined to their dormitory, and the study groups and "university courses" resumed once again.

The spring brought floods to the Delta region. The deluge seemed to engulf everything—camps, cornfields, grapevines, villages. The wildlife also became endangered by that first year's immense flooding. There was no safe haven for animals. The relatively protected dry land of the camp was fenced off. A few small islands were sticking out of the endless sea outside, and all the animals tried to take refuge there. Under this pressure of circumstances, the unthinkable happened. Reed wolves and rabbits, foxes and deer, weasels and wild boars—literally hundreds of the most irreconcilable species of animals—huddled together. The variety of birds, hovering over the islands and covering the few remaining trees, was a spectacle of Biblical proportions. With the islands close to camp, just outside the fence, it was fascinating to observe the animals' behavior in a cataclysm. It was Noah's ark. Probably many of the ministers "wrote" sermons inspired by this experience, although the outcome they would have wanted, that the animals reconciled with each other and survived as a "community," surely did not come to pass.

As the flood threatened the villages of Lipovan fishermen, the prisoners were ordered to reinforce the existing levees and build new dams. The reward for this slavery was the most desirable privilege bestowed so far, the right to send a postcard to their families. In it they were allowed to ask for a five kilogram care package. Although Imre was in poor health and suffered from daily migraine headaches, his desperate desire to hear from his family made him volunteer for the hardest job. He was taken for diking. They had to dig the earth out and carry it in wheelbarrows up high on top of the dike. The daily norm was three and a half cubic meters of digging. They left deep holes and trenches behind that filled with water causing many serious accidents. Digging was hard enough, but wheeling the dirt up twelve meters high on a narrow boardwalk, holding all that weight and keeping one's balance on a steep plank, was sheer idiocy for a feeble creature like Imre. He predictably failed to achieve the norm, which meant losing his postcard rights. He thought he had lost his last chance, his last hope, but human goodness prevailed. His young friends, seminary students from Kolozsvár, generously stepped in and helped him make his quota.

In the midst of Imre's strivings, he was blasted with an emotional bombshell—an official notice that Judit had divorced him. This was the only news to reach him in two years. Rationally at first, he found pragmatic arguments for Judit's decision. Perhaps the future well-being of their children was at stake. Perhaps she needed to pursue her own career and needed to be on her own to facilitate that. Maybe she had met someone who assuaged her loneliness and could share her life. After all, people divorced every day for many reasons. He pondered these possibilities briefly but dismissed them all, except for his children's welfare, as too uncharacteristic of his loving, loyal wife. Then he recalled the rumors prisoners had heard about pressure to get divorces which the Securitate had placed upon spouses of political prisoners. He also knew that merely imprisonment itself of a husband was sufficient legal grounds for a wife to obtain an automatic divorce. After due consideration he dismissed these arguments too, believing that Judit was strong enough to withstand the pressure and brave enough to withstand any hardships.

Imre then decided the notice had to be false. Prisoners had figured out that they were not allowed to receive loving letters from family and friends. Wives, children, parents and relatives spent hours every week writing about good things. The letters arrived containing heartfelt intimacies, expressions of thoughtfulness and hope, and details of the daily little successes in their lives. All these, the guards threw away. But let one letter arrive about sickness or injury, death or divorce, hardship or hopelessness, suffering or loss of faith, and that letter would be delivered. He hadn't received any news that might have explained or mitigated this divorce news. He also knew prison officials might well have printed the notice themselves. Imre wanted to believe he was being deceived or manipulated.

At the same time the idea of losing his family on top of the loss of his career, estate, freedom, health and dignity was simply more than Imre could take. He accepted the divorce as if it were true, and it was driving him crazy. His friend Rev. László Székely counseled him intensely. "Please stop thinking of your family all the time. Trust that they are alive and can manage their lives. You must survive seven years, and that is enough for you to worry about. You need all your energy to keep going." Imre managed to pull himself out of his irrational grief and concentrate on sending a postcard.

Thus, before Christmas of 1961, Imre triumphantly wrote his first postcard to Judit addressed to her parents in Székelykeresztúr. The text was restricted to a few lines and had to be written in Romanian. Any deviation would have resulted in the rejection of its mailing. The message might have read like this:

> My Dear Mother, Wife, Brothers, and Children!
> I am healthy. Don't worry about me. I have the right to receive a care package of 5 kilograms net weight. Please send 1 kg bacon, 2 kg melted butter in a plastic container, 1 kg sugar cubes, 1/2 kg cheese and 1/2 kg salami. Wrap well in plastic bags. In a separate package please also send 400 Marasesti cigarettes, toothbrush with paste, soap bar, 2 white flannel shirts and underpants, 1 pair of heavy-duty boots, 2 pairs of wool socks, a belt, and 2 handkerchiefs.
> Please don't send any letters and do not try to visit. Also, don't send any more packages until I write you again.
> I kiss you all with great love, Imre

He was ecstatic to receive the first care package by the next Christmas. The cigarettes in particular were "hard currency" in prison. His joy soon dissipated into disappointment, however, when he could find nothing personal from Judit or the children. His prison mates received tiny letters hidden in the melted butter or inside the salami. What happened to his family? In his next postcard Imre risked adding a bold allusion:""I haven't received *the* package from Siménfalva. Please, put my wife's and children's address on the package." A "sign" finally arrived in another package, Judit's home-woven towel with the family monogram. No hidden codes, nothing personal ever came.

Traps for Judit

After her husband's arrest Judit lived in terror of the secret police. Her very dreams seemed to be under surveillance. If theirs had been the "glass house" of a minister, now she was completely unprotected, exposed to winter weather of the merciless Securitate. She had no home besides the parsonage. Her first impulse was to stay with the congregation, her beloved extended family. The church's lay president and his wife, an elderly, childless couple, had became the loving parents she had always yearned for. The village collected money to support her family, but she declined to take it. Though such offers were greatly appreciated, she wanted to earn her living, not take alms. She played the piano and the church needed a music director, so she registered for a Unitarian music director training course in Kolozsvár. Her application, however, was never filed or answered by the Headquarters. The training started on the day of the trial, but she was not on the Headquarters' list. Clearly, they did not want the wife of Imre Gellérd and they did not care about his young children.

In due time the minister of the neighboring village signaled his desire to take over Imre's ministry. The congregation decided they were prepared to wait for seven years to get *their* minister back. Unfortunately, the village broke down under the pressure of church and state policy. The church had amended its policy so that politically imprisoned ministers would not be allowed to go back to the churches in which they had been arrested. Imre's former student, now his rival, became the candidate for the vacant pulpit of Siménfalva.

Judit had no desire or will to start life over again but she had no choice. She alone was responsible for her children and they would have to move. Struggling to overcome the paralyzing sense of victimization, she realized she needed to make some bold decisions. Her first step was a radical one: divorce her husband. Her impulse had a political as well as a personal dimension. The Securitate had reminded her that unless she became de facto head of her family and the breadwinner, she risked the chance that her children could be taken away from her and sent to an orphanage. As cruel as a divorce seemed after Imre's imprisonment, she remembered how unhappy their marriage had been for her. She had needed for more intimacy and attention. Her upbringing in sexual abuse imprinted the burden of inhibition and an ever present sense of guilt upon her. They both seemed to be illiterate in matters of intimacy. Sex was somehow a mere side effect of marriage, not a source of joy and closeness. Judit's shy attempts to express her desires and fantasies went unnoticed by Imre, or worse, brandied as "perversion," which humiliated her. They were perfect partners in sharing their ideas and their responsibilities for society and ministry; but as a woman, Judit had been very lonely in this marriage. She had resented the marriage then, and now she resented her betraying husband even more. Divorce was a simple unilateral dismissal of her imprisoned husband.

As a divorced woman and single mother, however, she faced repeated attempts of sexual harassment by the secret police agents. During required weekly appointments, certain Securitate officers tried to take advantage of her vulnerability. Men regarded her as a free prey, and it took all her might to protect herself within walls of strict chastity, which isolated her from any kind of socializing. She lost her trust in men, and the possibility of a second marriage became a distant one. Locked tight within her righteous and impenetrable walls of celibacy, relying on no one but herself, she proved to be stronger than the immoral system which she would fight for the next twenty years.

Evacuating the parsonage while having no place to go forced Judit to send her son to her stepmother. Judit was greatly concerned that the stepmother would turn her abuses against the boy too, but the best she could do was hope that the arrangement would be temporary. She needed a job badly, but she also wanted to be true to her dreams. With two children and no home or money of her own, the way back to medical school was closed for her. Yet she was reluctant to compromise her desire to study medicine a second time.

She finally decided to pursue her dreams. After much harassment and political maneuvering, she made it into a college for medical assistants and nurse practitioners, an unheard-of practice in that society at her age of thirty-three. She moved into a boarding school and took her son with her. Her young classmates respected and helped her. The tyrannical president was not so kind, deciding this convict's wife was just a Cinderella who wouldn't make it. With an iron will, however, Judit proved him wrong. She kept herself invulnerable and took the intended humiliations with grace and dignity. She worked three jobs to earn the equivalent of one meager salary. Three years later she graduated with her class and was invited to become a teacher at that school. Over the next two decades she trained nurses and nurse practitioners, and her teaching excellence was nationally recognized.

Judit's primary moral support through these years was her faith. She had never felt truly at home in her acquired, imposed religion. Her intellectual needs were met perfectly well by Imre's brilliant sermons, but she missed the ritual, the mystery, the communion of Roman Catholicism that satisfied her deep devotional needs. In 1963 she therefore took another radical step. She sought the advice of Archbishop Áron Márton, one of the holiest and most persecuted men in Transylvania who was still under house arrest after almost two decades. She asked him to take her back into the faith of her birth. Bishop Áron looked deeply into her eyes and blessed her. "Go now, your faith will keep you." This blessing meant life to Judit. She was able to take communion again! Religion became the pillar of her life. She went even further: she also made her eight-year-old son convert to Roman Catholicism. Although according to custom daughters follow their mother's religion and sons their father's, she broke with the tradition.

She considered it her right to raise her children in her faith. She also made an attempt to convert her daughter, but Zizi fiercely resisted. Zizi wanted to stay with her father's religion as an expression of loyalty to him. Seeing her strong will, Judit arranged with their friend Rev. Áron Török for Zizi's confirmation in the privacy of his parish in the remote village of Énlaka.

Coerced Suicide—a Clean Murder

After a few months of hell working on the dikes, Imre became overworked and excessively dystrophic, but he feverishly tried to hang onto his right to send postcards. One day he fell from the twelve-meter-high boardwalk into the deep mud and his wheelbarrow fell on top of him, badly bruising his groin. He was sent back to the Periprava camp needing hospitalization. Prisoner doctors had the right to refer extremely dystrophic inmates to a hospital or to prescribe a more nutritious diet, but the guards usually interfered with the doctors and stole the precious medicine to sell it in the prison or on the black market. An extreme case of injustice was that of Dr. Iacobescu, a caring, warm-hearted Romanian doctor. When he sent Prof. János Erdö to the hospital because of advanced malnutrition, the sergeant punished the doctor and divested him of his in-prison medical practice and privileges. Although Imre may have been dangerously malnourished, being sent for recovery was a punishment to him because he was prevented from earning postcard rights and thus news from home.

Another Christmas passed, the fourth year of isolation from his family and the world. One day a messenger arrived with some news for Imre. The news was very bad, the man warned. This man, unknown to Imre, told him in detail about a gruesome event he had just "witnessed" in Székelykeresztúr, the triple funeral for Imre's wife and his two children. Judit had allegedly committed an extended suicide, killing their two children before taking her own life.

Irme was inconsolable. The earth shattered and the sky burned, his grief was so unbearable. He concluded that his life was no longer worth living. He had seen prison mates end their suffering by throwing themselves onto the high-voltage electric fence. Feeling desperate, he ran at the fence. To his great disappointment, friends wrested him to the ground. They reminded him of the Securitate's well known method of torture by disseminating false information in order to drive prisoners to suicide. Suicide for the Securitate was a convenient and "clean" way to murder, and since he couldn't work and was a burden, he was a prime candidate to be "crossed off the list."

A deep despair took hold of Imre. He still had three more years ahead of him in this hell of uncertainty. His will to live was slipping away. He thought, if he just had some psychic ability, he could see his family. His thoughts were becoming more bizarre and less grounded in reality, and he knew it. Once he lost his mind, he mused, then there was truly nothing left.

❖ ❖ ❖

Judit's graduation gift from her school was a trip to the Black Sea. She took Zizi along. Their tour bus passed through the spectacular region of the Danube Delta. It was dawn. The misty mystery of the swamp and dancing reeds, the myriad of birds rising like golden clouds, evoked something of the unspoiled bounty of the time of creation. Zizi was lost in a reverie contemplating the intense beauty when suddenly barbed wires and watchtowers cut into the flesh of this realm. She stared as she felt the very earth agonize in its wounds. To Zizi's anxious question, her mother answered, "Yes, it is a prison camp." From somewhere Zizi knew that her father was alive.

CHAPTER 7

The Failed Attempt

T he time arrived for Rev. László Székely, sentenced for only four years, to say good-bye. According to practice, two weeks before completing his term, he was put on an enriched diet so that his skeletal condition would be a little embellished. He left his warm clothes and other valuables to Imre, his best friend, and promised to ask the Unitarian Bishop to intervene on his behalf. Imre's depression, insomnia, and headaches worried him. Székely's weeping over his own liberation was just another irony of that distorted world. He was not sure that he would ever see his friend again. "Please, Imre, hold on. I will free you. Just hold on one more year," he begged.

Rev. Székely's courtesy visit to the Bishop of the Transylvanian Unitarian Church was an unhappy memory. "Would you like, your Eminency, to hear about the rest of the Unitarian ministers still in prison?" "No, I wouldn't," was the cold reply." "They are mostly in decent health," Székely pressed on. "I don't want to hear," said the Bishop ready to burst in anger. "But please listen, your Eminency! Imre Gellérd's health situation is precarious. He still has three more years of his sentence. Please help him. Use your connections to free him, for he might not make it." "I don't care," said the Bishop. The Rev. Székely left the office crying bitterly.

Dying a Little at a Time

Spring brightened up life in prison a little bit. Chances came up for a desirable farming assignment at the Delta's cornfields and vegetable gardens. Though extremely weak and dystrophic, Imre volunteered again and was selected. The farm procession took off the next morning on the ten kilometer march. Barley fields on both sides of the trail made them covet the fresh greens. Risking punishment they grabbed a handful of green barley or plain weeds at the roadside and gobbled them up. During the coming year this illegal source of nutrition would keep them alive. Ironically, the malnutrition'seemed to cure Imre's chronic hepatitis.

In early spring a group of the prisoners from the Periprava camp was taken to hoe grapevines. This seemed like a blessing because they had

70

access to a delicacy, the pleasantly sour leaves and vine-shoots—of course, when the guards were not looking. They longingly hoped for a second hoeing opportunity when the grapes were about to ripen, but that would have been far too great a privilege for political prisoners. Instead they were assigned to hoeing corn. This was hard work, for the cornfields were reedy and the only tool they had to cut the tough reeds with was a dull hoe. The armed guards and their dogs dictated the work speed. Those who lagged behind were hit by the guards with their rifles and sticks. The punishment was occasionally worse—fifty pushups for people who could barely drag themselves to keep up with the intense rhythm.

If they considered hoeing corn exhausting work, something much worse awaited them—cutting reeds in the swamp. It was the greatest hardship in all of their prison years, and Imre was selected. Standing in water, very cold water during the spring and the fall, sometimes sinking into the marsh up to their knees or belt, they wrestled with the seven-feet-high reeds. There were snakes and leeches in the mud. Frogs as big as their boots would jump on them. It was terrifying to fall into the swamp, for that could mean instant drowning. As with so many other things in the prison, this activity had no meaning whatsoever. It was not about land reclamation. Romania had plenty of fertile land; the Delta had always been a wildlife refuge, a tourist attraction. Cutting reeds was simply a Sisyphean work of diabolic torture.

They were thirsty, dehydrated, and there was no potable water, so they had to drink the water of the swamp. They kept drinking it until the corpses of dogs and pigs first appeared in it. By then it was too late, and a raging epidemic of dysentery broke out in the prison camp. There was no adequate medical response at first and not enough medicine. Prisoners died, one after another, some simply because of dehydration. They held funerals each morning and each evening. As the number of bodies increased, the prisoners were ordered to dig the graves for the dead. Priests and ministers took turns conducting rudimentary funeral services, if allowed at all. Later the guards simply boxed up the bodies and took them outside of the camp. The boxes came back empty, for the next transport.

This was still not the worst. Typhoid fever began to take its victims. Now the number of the dead was so high that during the night the guards piled the bodies on horse carts and buried them outside of the camp in mass graves. The anxious inmates did not dare to look into each other's eyes. Who would die next?

Imre was next to fall ill. Already seriously dystrophic he collapsed with dysentery. There was barely any medicine left by then. All they had was carbon, and not in the form of pills but simply carbonized logs of wood. They ate as much of it as they could. It helped some, but Imre was losing the battle. He became so dehydrated that he could no longer get on his feet. That night the guards, making their routine rounds, saw no chance for him to recover and carried him to the "chamber of agony" to die. Prisoners considered to be "hopeless cases" were isolated from the rest, and no more medicine was wasted on them. That was prison medical ethics.

Imre was lying on the cold cement floor in his sweat and bloody excrement. His abdominal cramps were so violent that they probably prevented him from falling unconscious. He accepted his fate and tried to focus all his remaining energy to pray farewell to his loved ones and prepare for the unknown journey. He knew that his children, if they were alive, would never find his grave. He found deep comfort in God, who would finally free him from his suffering. His spirit was ready to return to its Creator. He vaguely sensed his neighbor's final death struggle. The night seemed an eternity. He had no more energy even to shiver, and his senses began to fail him.

God intended life for Imre. He woke up in the hospital. He was told later that the next morning when the guards and the physician on duty came to assess the deceased and erase them from the record, they found him still alive. That morning a good Samaritan, a Romanian-Jewish doctor was on duty. He pulled him out from among the dead bodies and had him placed in the prison infirmary. There he was re-hydrated and given some of the scarce medicine. Slowly he regained consciousness.

As he recovered Imre he began to worry about his obvious inability to continue the physical work in the swamp. He weighed thirty-six kilograms, less than eighty pounds. A truly divine intervention saved him again: he was selected for kitchen work. This seemed like heaven for him, even chopping wood and carrying heavy sacks of vegetables. The vegetables which they prepared for the cook were half rotted most of the time, but it was food! And nothing was to be wasted. Slowly he gained enough weight and energy to keep up with the workload. If any work could be called "enjoyable" in prison, he did enjoy working in the kitchen.

His privileged position granted him an effective way of "mass counseling," which infused his life with a new meaning. Every night when the band of deadly tired and ravenously hungry prisoners returned to the camp, Imre served them good news along with the food. Attributed to "reliable information," he made up stories, a new story every night. All of them were variations on the theme of their impending liberation. Even

Imre was inclined to believe his epiphanies. They were so hungry for good news that they easily suspended their rational minds to be nurtured by hope. The storyteller in Imre would find a grateful audience for many months to come. He was practicing a sort of brainwashing, indeed, but one with hope.

Re-education

In 1962-63 prison life underwent a significant change, and the change itself inadvertently awakened new hope in them. A new phase of their ordeal was introduced called "re-education." In the Danube Delta the guards held these sessions on the riverbank. Prisoners were divided into two groups, the clergy and other intellectuals in one, workers and peasants in the other. The guards drew the dividing line in the sand between them. Primitive-minded officers lectured the workers, pointing to the other group, which was to be blamed for their imprisonment.

There were many Jehovah's Witnesses among the prisoners. The very reason of their incarceration was their religion, regarded as a dangerous and fanatical sect. The prison leadership wanted them "deprogrammed." The best and most charismatic theologians were selected for the re-educational team. Rev. Richard Wurmbrand and Rev. Imre Gellérd were appointed as leaders of the team. The guards locked them up with the crowd of Jehovah Witnesses and said to themselves, "Let's see what happens." Rev. Wurmbrand was an extraordinarily charismatic person. He spoke some fourteen languages. A fine friendship evolved between the two of them. Being locked up in one room, they all had a unique chance to discuss ecumenical issues, and they didn't bother reprogramming the Jehovah's Witnesses.

In 1963 all prisoners from the Danube Delta were unexpectedly transported to the feared underground jail in Jilava. This fortunately lasted for only a short time before they were sent back to Szamosújvár once again. The main result for these transfers was their reassignment to work in the jail's factory.

Here, re-education took place in earnest. For the first time newspapers of the Romanian Communist Party were distributed among the inmates. Next, prison officials announced that those who "behave" might soon be released, and this appeal brought the wolf out of some prisoners. New cell supervisors were appointed from among the most "reliable" prisoners. These zealous informers surpassed the guards in their malice. They lived inside, knew every secret or misbehavior, and reported them. While guards were forbidden to enter the cell during the night, these informers were controlling and stealing even the inmates' dreams. They introduced a new reign of terror in their hope for an earlier release. But in a strange twist, prison officers deeply despised them and never did grant them privileges. Those footmen to the oppressors were released alongside those who resisted.

During this time the first books became available to the inmates, and films were shown to them—Chinese and Soviet films about the superiority of Communism. After five years of total isolation from the outside world, these movies were sensational! They saw the completely changed map of Africa for the first time. During movie time inmates were not allowed to look at each other; they had to steadily gaze at the screen.

The worst ordeal of re-education in Szamosújvár was called "the Kindergarten," a mockery of a trial used for ideological brainwashing and reprogramming. The prisoners were to be prepared for real life. These sessions typically consisted of a lecture by a Securitate officer. He would pathetically try to convince the inmates that the regime did not want to annihilate them, but that in fact the government loved and deeply appreciated all of them. Consequently, it was the inmates' turn to show repentance and gratitude for such love. All prisoners were expected to exercise sincere self-criticism and to assess their political crimes, which were committed perhaps out of ignorance. Their time served had granted an opportunity for them to take responsibility for those misdeeds. By admitting their guilt they also had a chance to apologize and sincerely promise that they would never again engage in such activities.

At that point in this daily routine, one of the prisoners was supposed to come forward to give a testimonial, thereby ending on a high note with expected repentance. The promise had to be concrete, a proof, an offering of worthiness for the grace of the Communist Party that would grant them liberation. This circus was nothing short of a coercion for moral self-prostitution, a final push to total demoralization. For those who had already been in prison for ten or fifteen years or were serving life sentences, the possibility of release was so acute that some of them lost their last drop of humanity. A disgusting race for favors began.

At one of these sessions a Hungarian prisoner volunteered and offered a memorable speech of "repentance" in which he openly accused the Communist regime and the Securitate themselves for their crimes. The officers gasped, and he received a cruel retaliation. But the rest of the prisoners, for the first time, felt their human dignity restored by this noble act of defiance. The air they were breathing became fresher. One man's moral courage and integrity was able to heal a hundred crippled souls.

The Crisis of Freedom

The last two weeks before release the prisoners were given not only a fattening diet but also one last attempt at political blackmail in an effort to recruit collaborators for the Securitate. Typically this would consist of an offer for a high-career job in exchange for one's services. If the offer was refused—"I don't like you, I have been your prisoner for years, you have taken away everything I had, how could I ever serve you?"—the prisoner was intimidated. "With you or without, we will build the Communist society. If you are a stumbling block for us, we have our methods to get rid of you, so you had better watch out!" was their ominous farewell.

In June, 1964, all the prisoners of Szamos·jv·r were gathered for a meeting with high-ranking military officers. One of them solemnly announced that the Communist Party had decided to grant its grace to all prisoners. By August 23, the national liberation day, all political prisoners would be released and assigned to jobs appropriate to each of them in a free society. The Party would guarantee their happiness, but they would have to prove themselves worthy by their enthusiastic contribution to the glorious socialist government in Romania.

The next two months in prison were spiritually more trying than the previous years but for a different reason. It was a time of joyful anticipation mingled with troubling doubts. They simply did not trust the Communists and feared that this was a trick or a trap. Besides, most of them had no information about their families, and the fear of uncertainty suddenly surfaced. Would they have the strength to face life if their loved ones had died? What if no one were waiting for them? Could they, perhaps, have been long forgotten? What would be their financial situation? What would be their "assigned job"? Where would "home" be? The prison became a very quiet place those last weeks. They had a hard time imagining what freedom would be like. A mixture of hope and fear weighed heavily upon them.

The day that they had been dreaming of finally arrived. The release process began, but nobody knew when one's day would be. Every morning they prepared anxiously, gathering together their few belongings and hiding treasured items under their clothes to take home as memorabilia.

The last bitter event of the correctional campaign was a "military court" game played just before their release. In this game the judge and prosecutors were role-played by prisoners, and the casting of the roles was done by the officials. The goal was to examine the inmates' level of re-education. The "play" court required that prisoners, once again, admit their political felony, exercise self-criticism, and promise loyalty to the cause of socialism. Imre categorically rejected this moral self-prostitution. He energetically denied any guilt or the need for ideological change. As punishment he was in the very last group to be released.

Where to Go?

Imre was released in August, 1964, with an allowance for a train ticket to his home. The prison truck dropped him at the railway station and left him there unguarded! Freedom suddenly became a serious existential crisis. "Where to go now?" His wife had divorced him, and she might have even died.

Those miles between the prison and his hometown were the longest miles he had ever taken. He had to walk about two kilometers from the train station in Székelyudvarhely to his mother's house. He barely made it, he was so weak and emotionally run down. Although he wore civilian clothes, his shaved head advertised his recent past. Though there were shaved heads everywhere in those days, people looked at him strangely. Some who did not know him expressed compassion; others, even former friends, crossed the street to avoid meeting him. The first shock in the dark and empty neighborhood was the disappearance of the old cottage where he grew up and where his mother had lived. It had been torn down and a new house, full of strangers, had replaced it. His heart almost stopped. A young couple, kissing in the shadow of the gate, showed the way to the house of Imre's oldest brother. He timidly opened the door and stuck his head in. Recognizing him and flying into his arms, brother Ferenc and his wife Berta screamed what Imre wanted to hear: "Everybody is alive! Everybody!" With such a wonderful welcome, he too became alive.

He found a haven in Ferenc's home. His good wife Berta lovingly cared for him. He was so weak that he could not walk alone. Two weeks had passed before he gathered enough courage and strength to visit Judit and his children. What was so painful that neither of them came to see him.

The changes in the outside world bewildered him. The deepest shock, however, came with the realization of the society's almost complete indifference toward him and others who had been absent from life for years. Now that he resurfaced, the world ignored him. Some people seemed to avoid him, pretending not to recognize him. It was true, he had aged so much that his own brother barely recognized him, but he was only forty-five. There were no welcoming words from his Church or from society, no recognition of his having lived through hell although committing no'crime, steadfastly resisting compromise, standing by his principles, and most of all, withstanding torture in order to save others from prison. Nobody said a "thank you!" to him. The indifference and ingratitude of the outside world called into question the value of his sacrifice on others' behalf. The same was true for the other former political prisoners; those who managed to preserve their moral integrity in the bowels of hell suddenly questioned the very meaning of their lives.

Embroidered Rags

Through it all, one heart continued to beat in the rhythm of her father's. Zizi was eleven when her father disappeared from her life. Now she was sixteen, and the news of her father's liberation meant as much anxiety as joy. "Will he recognize me? How will I ever be able to tell him the secrets of my heart and the events of those lost years? Will our family be re-united? How will my father cope with the shock of my mother's and brother's conversion to Roman Catholicism? Will my mother love my father any more?" she asked.

Then one day the door opened, and there was her father! He hadn't been able to walk by himself. Aunt Berta accompanied him to the maternal grandparents' house where Zizi had returned for a visit. Zizi barely recognized him. He was a broken, old man. His hair had turned white, he was emaciated, his face gray and wrinkled. And his eyes! There was no shine, no life in his eyes, only pain and suffering and fear. Like a beaten animal he seemed to lack the will to stand up straight and look into their eyes. His movements were slow and cautious as he struggled to keep his balance. What had happened to her proud, radiating, happy father!

"Zizi! Ziziiii!" he whispered with the passion of a prayer. His ecstasy was a mixture of a painful outcry and glorious ode. He folded his arms around her as if he never wanted to release her again. Zizi wanted that moment to last forever.

The little girl whose image the father cherished for years no longer existed. "You grew into a radiant young woman, so much like your mother when I first met her and fell in love with her! Your voice is so warm, so musical," he exclaimed in amazement. Her father presented his gift to her, his prison satchel and some tattered rugs, his prison clothes. Each piece had "ZIZI" embroidered on it. This was his prayer. He saw her name in the constellation of the stars during those dark, cold, lifeless nights.

Zizi had a surprise for her father too, playing her violin to him for the first time, so proudly! Those hundreds of hours of violin practice were all worth it, just for that moment of his tears of joy.

There was another cathartic encounter on that day. Imre's dream about meeting Judit once again, holding her in his arms, had kept him alive for most of those years. Now they were standing face to face, but as two strangers. Their realities were very different. There was an immense gap between the two of them and in their complete inability to approach each other in a loving, healing way. Their separate suffering now spilled over'and wounded the other. She expected him to recognize her heroism and chastity. He expected her to empathize with his suffering and to care for him still. Then she hurled her life-long frustration at him in the form of a hostile challenge: "Do you continue to view Dániel Simén, our destroyer, as a true man and your friend?" He wanted to believe that his friendship to his mentor had nothing to do with his political victimization by the system. "Yes, I do, I'm afraid...," he half replied. His answer was principled but fatal. Judit, perhaps not surprised, was bitterly triumphant. "In that case we no longer have a common ground on which to build a future together. I don't consider you a suitable parent and I must take sole responsibility in raising our children." The hope that had nurtured Imre's will to live now shattered before the reality of their separate lives.

Unforgiveness

All political prisoners in the late 1950's and early 1960's were sentenced under the ruling of the Communist Party's General Secretary Gheorghe Gheorghiu-Dej. In those years Romania had some fifty thousand political prisoners, mostly intellectuals. Imre served more than five years out of seven. Under international political pressure Gheorghe Gheorghiu-Dej pardoned all political prisoners in 1964. It was not an amnesty, so the second part of Imre's sentence, the additional five years of deprivation of his civil rights, remained like a dark cloud hanging over him. He was afraid and reluctant to apply for full rehabilitation even after the five years passed because implicit in that application was the recognition of his guilt. He was expected to ask for forgiveness and be re-tried by the same military court as a precondition for rehabilitation. Although his prison sentence #167/April 8, 1960 by the Military Court of Cluj on the charges of an attempt to undermine the social order, based on Art. 209 had long expired, yet for eleven more years Imre was technically not a free citizen. It was not until May 29, 1975, that he was finally granted formal rehabilitation by the Military Court of Cluj under Decision #290.

Rehabilitation is one thing, forgiveness is another. The system would never forgive him. Neither would his Church. He continued to remain stigmatized for the rest of his life.

* * *

Only as that generation later attempted to heal itself, did the Transylvanian Unitarian Church award the Reverend Imre Gellèrd with an earned *posthumous* doctorate in theology—twenty-five years after he had completed his dissertation and fifteen years after his death.

* * *

Eighteen Unitarian clergy were imprisoned between 1958 and 1964. Three of them were professors at the Protestant Theological School. Four were their students. Three of the Reverend Nyitrai family—husband and wife, both ministers, and their son, a seminary student—were imprisoned at the same time. The mother was sentenced to twenty-five years for a poem she wrote. The Reverend Imre Kelemen and his seminary student son were in prison together. The lives of family members in the prison were so carefully coordinated by the Securitate that they almost never met each other.

This is the complete list of the incarcerated Unitarian clergy. They all survived prison. A commemorative monument in the village of Nagyajta [Aita Mare] was erected in year 2000 by the local Unitarian congregation.

Prof. Dr. János Erdö - 4 years prison term [now dead]
Prof. Dr. Mihály Lörinczi - 7 years [now dead]
Prof. Dr. Dániel Simén - 7 years [now dead]
Rev. Dr. Imre Gellérd - 7 years [now dead]
Rev. Mór Rázmány - 1 year [now dead]
Rev. Mózes Nyitrai - 10 years [now dead]

His wife, Rev. Berta Deák, Mrs. Nyitrai - 25 years [now dead]
Their son, Rev. Levente Nyitrai, then a seminary student - 6 years
Rev. Imre Kelemen - 15 years [now dead]
His son, Csongor Kelemen, then a seminary student - 15 years
Rev. Mihály Végh - 15 years [now dead]
Rev. László Székely - 4 years [now dead]
Rev. Ferenc Bálint - 5 and half years [now dead]
Rev. Dezsö Szabó - 20 years [now dead]
Rev. Aron Léta - 10 years
Rev. Albert Pálffy - 6 years [now dead]
Rev. Ágoston Benedek, a seminary student - 4 years [now dead]
Rev. Balázs Sándor, then a seminary student - 25 years
Although not a clergyman, Dr. Elemér Lakó, a scholar and librarian
  of the Unitarian College Library and Archive - [now dead]

CHAPTER 8

Unwelcome

Freedom exposed Imre to new miseries. He had no income, no savings, no place of his own. Some of his clothing and his writings were all that Judit was able to save for him. She was no longer his wife, and Imre needed to regain the inner strength to face the reality of a separate life. Paradoxically, his inner reserves were depleted after he had arrived home. He needed to create new meaning to survive.

While in prison Imre and other writers around him were consumed by a burning desire to write. They had so much to write about. With paper and pen denied to them and with the complete deprivation from outside information, the capacity of their brains to bring up the richness of stored memories was nothing short of miraculous. Their minds were their "library." They were amazed by the extent of their memories, and how refined their intuitive functions became. The promise of the new meaning in freedom was the chance to write, finally.

Once the hermetically sealed world of prison opened, however, their memories played a cruel joke on them. Perhaps as a self-protective mechanism to get rid of the pain and suffering, their brains eradicated all the wonderful systems of ideas and data that were so carefully memorized. Such selective memory loss was a consistent complaint among the former prisoners. Unfortunately, few of them had the discipline and the courage— courage most of all—to put their experiences and ideas into writing immediately upon liberation.

The most disappointing reality he had to face was the irreversible loss of Siménfalva, *their home.* He was banned from what in his mind was his holy place. During the years in hell, Siménfalva grew into a sublime, heavenly reality, the recurring essence of his dreams, the clear spring that recharged his spirit in the total hopelessness. Now his grief over his shattered family was so unbearable that he wished he were long buried in an unmarked grave under the willows of the Danube.

After a few months of physical recovery Imre asked his Bishop for a parish assignment. He was sent to Homoródszentmárton [Martinis], which turned out to be a "punishment church" for Imre.

It would be a mistake to think that all villages are essentially equivalent. There are radical intellectual and spiritual differences even among neighboring villages. Sometimes it has to do with genetic roots because of centuries-long inbreeding in some of the isolated villages. Imre's pre- and post-prison congregations represented two extremes. Siménfalva, with its open-minded, intelligent people, eagerly embraced learning and growth. They appreciated their minister's efforts for their spiritual and intellectual well-being. That village was full of potential and most of its youth went on to higher education. Homoródszentm·rton, on the other hand, lacked that inner potential. Its people seemed insensitive to beauty and values of the intellect. They lacked vision. This was an earth-bound and destitute community. Having a Unitarian minister whose preaching they considered too "high," made them unaccustomed to attending church. Those few who came usually slept through the sermon. Imre was a disturbance to their unchallenged torpor.

Nobody wanted Imre there. The Reverend Sándor Zoltán, a prestigious scholar who had ministered to this village for fifty years, was intellectually and physically still vigorous. He did not show the slightest intention to retire, although he had long preached his scholarly treatises to an empty church. When Bishop Elek Kiss brought attention to his age, alluding to his overdue retirement, Rev. Zoltán responded, "As your Eminency recalls, we are the same age, former classmates. If you feel apt to govern the entire Church of Transylvania, I similarly feel capable to minister to a small village." The Bishop was disarmed by this argument, so the Church used Imre to unseat Rev. Zoltán. He was ordered to take over the pulpit from him in a coup-like manner. The congregation wouldn't have minded the change, but out of a sense of decency they did not welcome Imre. Interestingly, Rev. Zoltán did. Instead of seeing a rival or an enemy in him, he understood Imre's precarious situation. He became Imre's father, his elder brother, his intellectual partner. He wanted to help his colleague heal. For a while they stayed together in the parsonage, for he had no house of his own in which to retire. It was hardly possible for Imre to experience very much joy in his new freedom and new beginning in the face of such unfair treatment of this noble soul.

How different his first sermon of resuming his ministry was from those he had prepared during the prison years! Instead of rejoicing over a sacred covenant, Imre he had to apologize to his new congregation for wanting to serve them. His whole being protested against becoming the minister of Homoródszentmárton! Friends urged him to quit the ministry altogether and try to start a new career. He had plenty of other academic qualifications, they argued. But Imre's loyalty toward his Church was unbroken and unshakable; he wanted to free people from the mud of indifference. On that memorable first day in his new parish, he summed up his principles in his journal entry about that occasion:

I am at my new place. The fresh whitewash in my room hasn't dried yet. Everything around me is new. I am standing at the threshold of my new life. Mine is the experience of Mount Horeb, and I am filled with anxiety about the tomorrows. Will I be able to embrace the challenges? Doubts torment me, strategies chaotically swirl inside me. I cannot bear chaos. There is no way that I could go to sleep my first night here without making relative order among principles and plans.

Principles are primary. If the principles are clear, they will precipitate plans; and where there are principles and plans, there is order and prosperity. What should my guiding principles be in my new life?

First, I am not a beginning, but a continuation. I only join in the long labor of Christian pastors; my role is to assure the conditions of the continuity. I must therefore clearly assess the values which I am expected to safeguard and pass on to the next generation. My goal is two-folded, to cultivate those values in my congregation, and to enrich the heritage of which I am in charge. I must become a reliable, strong link in the chain of centuries of ministry. I must build on what my ancestors have accomplished. I must believe in my essential role in creating the conditions for the progress of my people.

I tremble under the weight of the responsibility. If I ever had to lose everything in life, I pray to God to spare this last treasure, my faith in the constructive effect of my work. I can serve only as long as I believe in the importance of my work in chiseling people to make them more human. I must be convinced that my contribution, although modest, is needed and even indispensable. A new principle results from this, that my Unitarian faith, by its very nature, must never be an impediment in the way of progress. My ministry to people must continuously contribute to the growth and prosperity of the community. I will be the engine and the wings for those who wish but cannot fly. I will be a bridle for those who are carried away by destructive passion. I will harness frenzied selfishness and hatred.

Doubts still keep my soul disquieted. Will I be a burden to my parishioners? Are religion and church truly desirable values, or are they an imposed burden upon people? I want to believe that this burden is a blessed one. I wish to be a burden like wings for a bird, like the motor for a car, like bread for a traveler, like the unborn child for a mother.

One is a giver and a taker at the same time. I too will offer to and accept from my congregation. The two must always be in balance. If I give less than I receive, their sacrifice is an alms for me. I pray to be able to always give more in spiritual treasures than I receive in material ones.

I look out through my windows. The stars are watching over my village, which from now on is my new home. I did not choose to live here; God sent me to this place for a purpose. The houses, the narrow streets, the orchards, the fields are wrapped in an heavy, cold silence. My parishioners slumber. They are renewing their strength to work for their daily bread, which they share with me.

How ironic some of his concerns were, echoing charges from his prison re-education about the parasitic nature of ministry and religion. Yet it was the social aspect of his humanity that had suffered most.

Healing Alone

Imre started his new life with a suitcase worth of old cloths and a box of his writings. He moved into the century-old parsonage which had probably never been refurbished. The crumbling walls, mice-infested rooms and attic, and the lack of a bathroom and furniture were anything but a welcoming home. He had absolutely no money. Judit gave him some of her scattered dowry, pieces of their beautiful furniture from Siménfalva, along with the grand piano. Her mother contributed to his empty kitchen. Villagers went through their rummage and donated everything from old furniture to chickens, from hand-woven rugs to dishes. Two odd beds, a small table for a desk, a couple of odd chairs, a wardrobe, a mirror and a few dilapidated bookshelves made his only room finally cozy. It perfectly symbolized his newly restored life from its ruins.

The two most dreaded conditions, cold and loneliness, were with him every day. As winter approached, his room turned into an ice chamber. The only source of heat was an old cast iron kitchen stove that did not keep up the heat; it had to be constantly fed with firewood and rekindled every time he arrived home. On winter mornings when he got up, the water was frozen in the bucket inside the house. The outdoor latrine was back in the courtyard and, unless there was moonlight, he groped through the mud in pitch darkness to reach it. Imre suffered from chronic cholitis with frequent diarrhea episodes and had to make many trips there during freezing nights. The paralyzing cold lasted for five months. The parsonage of Siménfalva, which had no electricity, was a luxurious mansion compared to that miserable place in Homoródszentmárton.

His first winter season passed without a salary, so families took turns in bringing food to their minister. In most households a fattened pig was killed each winter to feed the family throughout the year, and it was traditional to offer a generous portion to the neighbors, including the minister. Imre smoked raw sausages and bacon in his attic to preserve them for summer. The main food in his house was eggs that were generously produced from the various kinds of donated chickens. A dinner for guests was usually a dozen scrambled eggs served with pickles.

In the spring Imre planted fruit trees all over the large parish garden and cemetery—apple, pear, cherry—and some red and black currant bushes. His vegetable garden provided beans, egg plants, tomatoes, bell peppers, onion, parsley, dill, lettuce and potatoes, enough for his needs and of his neighbors'. Flowers were his real pride. Women of the village came to admire them and ask for seeds. He planted the most lavish and colorful varieties around the parsonage and in the church garden. Something was always in bloom from early spring until late fall. In the monotonous routines of village life, the colors meant life for him.

Autumns turned him into a poet and adventurer. He was fascinated by heights, so while picking apples, he climbed each tree to see the color-pageantry of the foliage from above. He covered every surface in the parsonage with the treasured apples, his fragrant "vitamin pills" for long winters. His pleasure of chasing heights proved especially useful when the young storks occasionally fell from their nest on the parsonage's tall chimney. Imre had to take the big chicks back in his arms, climbing up on the longest ladder.

Making traditional plum preserves—enough for several years— was a romantic social time of attending the campfire and stirring the marmalade for a whole day and night. Women attending the fire took turns in storytelling and singing under the starry sky. The highlight of the fall was the last Sunday of September, the Unitarian Harvest Thanksgiving celebration. The church was decorated with bunches of grapes and a wreath of wheat as a chandelier. "New bread" from the freshly harvested wheat would be served as communion bread.

Imre loved the fall season up to when that first killer frost massacred the flowers in his garden, turning his dahlias into black skeletons and his ripened grapes into ice pearls. The first frost was a day of mourning for Imre. It left him with the longing for the hot summer days, when he would swim up to his waist in fragrant grass and wildflowers and, as a mental exercise, he would call each weed by its Latin botanical name.

Village ministers traditionally received their salaries in the form of produce, wheat and corn, but only once a year. A token state salary was added to that to their peril. In 1948, during the nationalization of church properties, the Unitarian Church had made an unfortunate compromise with the Romanian Communist state. It accepted salary subsidies for its ministers. The token state salary was not worth the price of the implied political entanglement of the Church with the state. This made the Unitarian Church ever more vulnerable. The Roman Catholic Church and its uncompromising leadership, for example, flatly refused this "generosity" and thus was able to keep its independence.

Many villages were too poor to pay their ministers their due remuneration. Imre received less than half of what he was entitled to get. Since the price of the cereals varied, one way of boosting it was raising hogs for the market. It was a difficult and risky business, but Imre's poverty forced him to undertake it. He had to cook huge kettles of potatoes twice a day for the pigs, though he did not have time to cook for himself. It seemed worthwhile when the first sets of piglets were born. After six weeks Imre packed the piglets into a horse cart and traveled all night to reach the market by dawn in Old Romania. That first business trip, however, ended in disaster. First, he sold his cargo way below the invested value of the feed. Then he lost all his earning to a pickpocket. He actually caught the thief, but when he reclaimed his money, an aggressive gang of Romanian Gypsies suddenly surrounded him, and he barely escaped a thrashing.

A source for additional income was Transylvania's "hard currency," the infamous fiery drink *szilva-pálinka,* a double distilled plum brandy. His garden and the cemetery were full of plum orchards. Although the beauty of their springtime blossoms was exhilarating, the distillation of the brandy was equally dreadful. Once the distillery opened in the neighboring village, it was booked for months. It took him two days and two nights of continuous work to produce the brandy. Sleep deprivation and the alcohol-saturated air in the windowless building always made him very sick.

Once he had the treasure, he was doomed to contribute to the continuous inebriation of his own people. Social drinking had always been heavy in Transylvania, as in the rest of Eastern Europe, and central to social life. Times of sadness, times of joy, and anything in between involved drinking *pálinka*. A farmer's greeting, "I wish you a brandied good morning," reflects this culture. Many who otherwise would not drink alcohol, such as ministers like Imre, were socially pressured to do so. Every parishioner who visited him—and one followed on the heels of another all day long—expected at least a glass of brandy and expected the minister to drink with them. Health reasons or other excuses were not appreciated and were rather interpreted as an insult. Imre had to use tricks, pretending to drink along while keeping his glass full. When the plum trees were barren, he had to buy the brandy, for any business with officials implied the expected bribery.

Making wine was just as essential to every household. People made wine from just about anything, occasionally even from grapes! Concord grape vines grew on trellises at every courtyard, but the real wine delicacy was the sweet, ruby-colored wine made of raspberry, red current or sour cherry, with lots of sugar. The black currant, unenjoyable as a fruit, made *vinum ferri,* with its rich iron content. It was *the* folk remedy for anemia, and it soon appeared on the pharmaceutical market in Germany.

While village ministers could rarely afford vacation away from their parish, Imre wouldn't give up for anything the much anticipated get-away in the Hargita mountains to pick wild raspberry. He moved into a mountain cabin and from dawn to sunset filled his buckets with the sweet and fragrant fruit. He processed the fruit on site and brought home raspberry preserves that filled his pantry and gallons of juice which soon fermented into the most fragrant wine. Berry picking, as enjoyable as it seemed, was not risk free because of the large population of brown bears and an occasional viper. Still, lovely days alone in the sunny wilderness were the best time for healing and meditation for him.

All of his activities combined did not provide enough real currency, so Imre decided to expand his farming operations. The church's farmlands had been confiscated by the Communist state, leaving the small vegetable garden and orchard. So Imre rented a few acres back from the collective farm. As a "class enemy" he was usually assigned the worst lot near the creek, where floods often wiped out his corn and sugar beet crops. When he was blessed with a good harvest, the collective taxed it heavily, barely leaving anything for the producer.

Farming for Imre was a self-healing, work therapy that helped him fight depression. He thought out whole systems of ideas while working in the field. He wrote entire theses in his head, as he did in prison. Working with his hands also gave him an opportunity to minister to his parishioners beyond the church walls. Sweating in the fields was an expression of his solidarity with his congregation. He wanted to live what he preached. Many elderly widows, unable to work their household lots, needed his help. He outworked most farmers; he had been well trained by watchdogs and prison guards. His parishioners were able to relate best to this aspect of his ministry, and it created a strong bond among them.

Typically Bankrupt

When Imre arrived there in 1965, Homoródszentmárton was a typical Transylvanian village that was bankrupt after a decade of collective farming. Farmers left the villages to work in factories of cities as far away as Bucharest or commuted to the neighboring Székelyudvarhely. City industry seemed more promising than collective farming. Of course, they did not have a choice between factory labor *or* farming. They had to do both.

Most of the women in the village worked in clothing factories in a weekly rotation of three shifts, commuting on dusty old buses over bad roads. At 4 a.m. women of all ages gathered at the bus stop on the roadside, exposed to the elements of occasionally minus 30 degrees Celsius. The buses did not always show up, so they tried to hitchhike to work or back home. There were Christmas Eves when mothers did not make it home from the factory by midnight, and their anxious families went to bed without a celebration. Dictator Nicolae Ceausescu had banned the observance of religious holidays anyway. Sundays and holidays were the "make-up" production time for those days when, for the lack of electricity or supplies, workers spent their entire eight-hour shift doing nothing. Once home from the factories, women plunged into their home shifts. During farming season they worked in the fields alongside their husbands or parents. Raising their children, managing the household and caring for the animals were the women's distinct responsibilities. By the end of the harvest season, exhausted, they appeared years older than their ages—and a generation older than their Western peers.

Men who were skilled in carpentry and masonry sought employment in the construction industry all over the country. Large city projects siphoned the men out of the villages, leaving the land to the women and old people, or letting it go unfarmed. The newer generation was losing the deep connection to the ancestral land. In the "good old times" farming was a dignified profession and granted a good living. In those times tradition ruled community life and the church was its centerpiece. The villages were prosperous. Such times ended in the 1950's. The country's agriculture was made hostage to central planning, while centuries-old local wisdom and experience were disregarded. The hilly country of Transylvania was utterly unsuited for large-scale, mechanized farming with heavy machinery. The collective ruined the prosperous agriculture of Transylvania within a decade. "Comrade engineers" were sent from Old Romania to supervise agricultural production in the small villages of Transylvania. They seemed to be ignorant and cared even less about what the right crops were in that region and how to keep the soil fertile.

Villagers were suffering over the dictated dilettantism and the consequent crop failures. They were powerless against the system. The rental cost of heavy machinery exceeded the value of total production. After having toiled all summer long and harvested the crops, they helplessly stood by as state trucks took most of the produce as payment for machinery and taxes. Token sacks of grains were usually the share left for the farmers. Sometimes collective crops were left unharvested in the confusion of central dictates, but the villagers were forbidden to gather the grain for themselves and their animals. Their precious crops had to be left to rot. The newspapers and the radio, nevertheless, continually reported "great victories and grand successes in increasing production" in agriculture and industry. Phony statistical data shamelessly claimed the unprecedented prosperity of their country and the superiority of socialism.

Self-sufficiency formerly meant harvesting one's own firewood from the family forest. This was selective harvesting par excellence. With the forests nationalized, people had to pay for firewood. The poor could not afford it and burned twig and cob instead. At the same time the state devastated their forests by clear-cutting and exporting the precious assets. The same ruthless practice managed their rich natural gas resources. The people had to use firewood while the natural gas from under them was sent to the Soviet Union. Imre's good parishioners secured his firewood, and he felt guilty for it.

The Bells of Time

The Unitarian congregation's concept of church growth lay exclusively in building projects, not in the area of the spiritual. They built something each year—for its spiritual effect. Raising money from egg sales and tea-and-cookie parties was a painstaking process every time, but they managed to restore the church sanctuary and the bell tower. Imre also wished for a bathroom in the parsonage, but his congregation never considered it a necessity.

One single person was capable of the mighty job of repairing the steeple, the Unitarian Rev. Dénes Benczö. He had climbed most of the Unitarian bell towers in Transylvania that needed repair. The whole village held its breath, watching him hang from a single rope on the hundred-foot-tall steeple and work for days to change the tiles and reset the globe and lightening rod. Imre held the other end of the rope from the ground.

One of the two bells in Homoródszentmárton was donated by its sister Unitarian Church of Montclair, New Jersey, in 1923. The story went back to the 1920's when Dr. Louis Cornish, then President of the American Unitarian Association, had reported the devastating consequences of the Treaty of Trianon on Transylvania's Hungarian minority. This report made American Unitarian churches aware for the first time of the oppression of Romania's ethnic minorities. A sister church project grew out of this awareness. For a few years American churches sent gifts, including several bells to Transylvanian churches that had lost their bells. During the Hungarian Revolution for Independence from Austria in 1848, and again during World War I, the bells had been melted down for cannons.

Transylvanians would not accept a church without bells. Bells were essential in the life of a community. Their role was "to call the living, to bury the dead, and to toll the alarm in times of storm, flood, fire, and invasion of enemies." When the regular bells rang, men took off their hats and rested for a moment in prayer. During thunderstorms and hail, bells "broke the storm clouds." Bells announced the sad news of a death in the village, and alarm bells called for community action. Transylvania's bells tolled the alarm during Mongol and Tartar invasions in the thirteenth century, Ottoman Turk attacks in the fifteenth century, and Austrian tyranny in the seventeenth century. In those times the bells warned people to find refuge within the walls of the church, to store their food in its bastille. Tolling a bell was an art. It had its own language which everyone understood.

Imre's church in Homoródszentmárton, although a traditional medieval fortress with walls and bastille, had a relatively new "Unitarian style" sanctuary—airy, luminous, with white-washed walls and large windows. Imre made a stunning discovery in his parish archives. He found the minutes of the congregation's historic meeting in the late nineteenth century, which revealed the fate of the original gothic church. "We disliked the ugly long faces of the saints on the painted walls (fifteenth century frescoes!), so we decided to demolish the church and build a new one, a veritable Unitarian house of worship, big and bright." So they did. While the walls of this national monument had fallen to a Turkish Ottoman siege, its sanctuary fell to a lack of historical consciousness. Its American bells completed the ensemble of the centuries.

Since churches had traditionally been havens for safeguarding their cultural traditions, Imre decided to express local tradition in the decoration of his church. He painted traditional archaic folk motifs on the furniture as a thanksgiving offering for his liberation from prison. If a bathroom was an unnecessary luxury in the parsonage, the congregation appreciated the luxury of decoration for the church. His pet project, a Székely carved gate in front of the church, found enthusiastic support. The tall and intricately carved gates were "status symbols" of their Székely [Secler] identity. The motifs of the carving were variations of basic Székely symbols—the Sun, the Moon and the tree of life. The two pillars were twelve feet tall, with pigeon holes on the roof and an inscription, "Peace to the entering, blessings to the departing." A Székely gate would last for two or three centuries. Erecting traditional gates, decorating homes and churches with embroidery, carvings, and painted furniture were expressions of people's cultural identity and ancient heritage as well as of a protest against Communist monoculture.

CHAPTER 9

Crises and Opportunities

I mre's vision to reform his church sprang from the very beginning of his new ministry. He began to introduce the programs that had been so successful in Siménfalva. He tried to motivate his congregation to attend church. He preached his best sermons. Though walls of indolence surrounded him, he was stubbornly confident that transformation would eventually come about in his dormant congregation.

Ministry in a village was complete and complex involvement in people's life. In fact, the minister was expected to act as *the* leader of and advisor to the community in just about every problem of daily life. Imre practiced a pro-active form of pastoral care. He ceremonially visited each family in his parish once a year. These were intimate family worship services, followed by extended conversation about their lives and unsolved problems. His interest in medicine found good use, for people would consult their minister before their doctor. Helped by Zizi's medical connections, Imre arranged consultations at the best clinics and best specialists and found scarce medicine for his parishioners. He tested them psychologically, using Rorschach and other personality tests, so he could work with them better.

People craved attention and loved celebrations, so he turned church life into a series of rituals and festivals. Although the adults remained passive spectators during their children's performances, at least the children and youth caught fire. The children were his allies.

In the background of Imre's everyday toil, his desire to transcend the suffocating walls of marginalization, to enrich his church's theological and historical self-image, became irresistible. The reissuing of the Unitarian theological journal, the *Keresztény Magvetö [Christian Seed Sower]*, banned by the communists, was a new promise for him. The journal was his chance for his long-cherished plans for church renewal. He sent a whole series of essays on practical theology for publication. He thought the pulpit in particular needed some overhauling. Fear of the Securitate had stifled the voice of the pulpit. Unitarian sermons became embarrassingly shallow, and the overgrown "language of flowers" needed much weeding. Preachers needed to find a clear, new direction which would be worthy once again of the Unitarian homiletical heritage. Only it this way would they provide real nourishment of hope to their congregations. Imre's time as a scholar and teacher seemed to have arrived finally. He kept writing fervently and the *Keresztény Magvető* published some of his papers.

Yet he wanted more. In March, 1968, he asked the Rector of the Protestant Theological School to consider his requalification for the doctoral degree, since he had already fulfilled his coursework and his dissertation had been already accepted before his imprisonment. The prison sentence fortunately did not wipe out his master's degree. He had a solid case, he was told. As it happened, however, his official correspondence with the Rector was handled—and answered—by none other than Vilmos Izsák, his betrayer, then the General Secretary of the Protestant Seminary. To Imre's humble request to the Rector, Izsák's response was: No! No requalification, no validation of his dissertation!

Before he lost heart, however, another possibility arose in February, 1969. The prestigious pulpit at Marosvásárhely [Tirgu Mures], the great cultural center of Transylvania, became vacant. Both of Imre's children were studying in that city, Zizi a second-year medical student and Andor a freshman in a technical school. Imre's longing for his family and his thirst for a cultured environment were great attractions. The three of them began to dream about living together—as a family!—in the elegant parsonage on Rigó street. His children were ecstatic about the posh place. Imre convinced himself that the pulpit of this great city, although a compromise to a faculty position at the Kolozsvár Seminary, was an acceptable alternative.

His chances to be elected were highly promising. The match was just right. The congregation of educated, middle class people wanted a scholar-minister. A unanimous vote by the congregation was a distinct possibility. Imre and his children lived in happy anticipation for weeks, although they all knew that the Bishop had the last word. Would the Bishop veto his election? Surprisingly, he was the Bishop's choice! He had one condition though, that he should remarry. Nothing would have been more agreeable with Imre.

Irony in Grief

While Imre waited for the crucial phone call about the outcome of his election, another phone call intruded into his life: the news of the sudden death of his mentor Dr. Dániel Simén. Pulmonary embolism, a complication of a bone fracture when he slipped in church, killed him within minutes. He died with Imre's name on his lips—asking Imre to bury him. He had never experienced a loss of that magnitude before. Simén had betrayed him and dragged him into prison, but Imre had long forgiven him. They spent five years in hell together and they survived. Imre asked him the "*Why?*" only once.

It was only now, in the light of the ironies in the deceased's last wish, that Imre was able to face the realities of their relationship. On the one hand, Dr. Simén's last wish was his last gift to his loyal friend, bestowing the chance for him to preach from the historic pulpit of Kolozsvár, a pulpit banned to Imre by jealous church authorities. On the other hand, Simén had asked for a eulogy from him that would be seen as an altar to his pride and their friendship, in the presence of Simén's rivals and enemies.

Imre's eulogy did indeed torture the ears of church leaders, reminding them of their intense dislike for his deceased father figure. Imre said he wished Dr. Dániel Simén had outlived him. He took his farewell saying, "Good bye, my Professor. What I am today is your creation. What I could have become is your dream. Thank you for being in my life. And though I feel that I am burying part of myself along with you now, I will try to be worthy to your legacy. We meet in the beyond." He said these words in the pulpit of the venerable Francis Dávid.

In his personal grief everything about his campaign for the Marosv·s·rhely pulpit became utterly unimportant. He eventually lost the election after a group of the Marosvásárhely congregation campaigned against him. With precise maneuvering, led by an attorney and lay president of the church, the pulpit was offered to Imre's friend. Marosvásárhely was another dream that eluded him. He was more sorry for his children than for himself, for he felt he had betrayed them. Later that same attorney, in another role, blocked Imre's chances for a faculty appointment at Kolozsvár.

Underestimated Determination

Zizi did not let her father dwell in sorrow over his grief and failure. At her urging he decided to insist on his rematriculation to the doctoral program and to rewriting his dissertation. This was also his scholarly obligation, since in his master's thesis he dealt with only the first three centuries of Unitarian intellectual history. It was utterly incomplete without the nineteenth century. For this reason he was strongly advised by his professors not to choose a different topic, but to rework his "old" dissertation. In about a year he was ready with it. Now a nerve-racking waiting period started again. It took state and church officials almost another year for just an in-principle decision whether or not his dissertation was acceptable. Finally, the answer came. At least it was not a rejection. Officials, Imre was told, would not even touch his work unless it was first translated into Romanian! The dissertation was 400 pages long; the official language of the Unitarian church was Hungarian; and freedom of religion was guaranteed by the Romanian Constitution. Yet Imre was ordered to do something that no one had ever done in his Church's history. Those who plotted against him, underestimated his determination, and he began the translation without delay. He was fluent in Romanian, his second language, and to render his dissertation into an eloquent Romanian was just a matter of time. With his busy parish responsibilities and farming, he had only the nights for scholarship. His chronic insomnia again was of some use. In February, 1970, he submitted his new dissertation in two languages, in two bulky volumes. Judit had typed his master's thesis on their old typewriter with carbon papers. This time Prof. Lajos Kovács' wife Klára did the honors.

While waiting for a response, Zizi kept infusing new energy into her father to reach for new and higher goals. Her ways were so persuasive that she occasionally managed to overpower his reluctance for change. In the arsenal of Imre's hopes, the possibility of a foreign scholarship was one of the most desirable. He was eminently qualified for it, having created serious scholarly works, knowing seven languages and being fluent in four. There had been two scholarships offered to the Transylvanian Unitarian Church during Imre's ministry: one to Oxford, England, and the other much later for Meadville/Lombard School of Theology in Chicago, Illinois.

The Bishop, ruling out any fair competitions, reserved for himself the exclusive right to handpick the candidates. Imre was not chosen; but the minister selected and sent to Oxford had no scholarly background or ambition whatsoever, and he used the opportunity to defect the country, fleeing to Austria. A huge political scandal followed this unprecedented incident. The Church lost face and any further scholarships. In fact, for the next decades, ministers were denied permits to travel to the West.

If this new failure to win a scholarship was not enough, the real disaster soon followed. Vilmos Izsák was appointed to the faculty position of Practical Theology in 1969—the very job for which Imre had aspired and prepared for more than a decade. He was doomed to witness how collaboration with the secret police bore fruits for Vilmos Izsák once again, while the system poisoned Imre's chances again and again.

Imre waited for a response from state officials for another year before he went to Bucharest to the Ministry of Cults in November, 1970, to find an answer himself. What he learned was stunning: everything was tied up by Imre's Church. The Ministry referred him back to his local "inspectorate" at the Unitarian Church Headquarters. The officials at Bucharest promised him their prompt cooperation if his church's arbitrators in Kolozsvár gave them a green light. Of course, Imre's church officials had "carefully" missed a particular deadline and were reluctant even to discuss his chances. Once again, all correspondence went through Vilmos Izsák. Allegedly Bishop Elek Kiss urged both offices to issue the permit for the doctorate, but Imre received only promises.

Finally, after a one-and-a-half year delay, the dissertation, which had been praised by scholars of several denominations as "the most brilliant work of the century," was accepted by the government office responsible for church affairs. Thus, twelve years after the first submission the Church set the time for the formal defense of his dissertation and a predictable conferring of the degree in the fall of 1971.

What happened next was nothing short of surrealistic. In July, 1971, a political thunder-storm, the so-called "cultural revision"—reminiscent of China's noxious cultural revolution—hit Romania. In essence this decree was the institution of hard-line Communist policy, a leap forward in dictator Ceausescu's iron rule to curtail cultural and human rights. All aspects of cultural and religious life were "revised" and draconian rules instituted to stamp out any democratic spirit and openness.

This was a triumphant moment for Vilmos Izsák. With diabolic consistency he continued digging Imre's grave. Being insider to the Department of Cults in Bucharest and the Securitate, he suggested that Imre's dissertation should fall under the revision. There was a sentence in the dissertation, he suggested, which could serve as the basis for his elimination from the doctoral program, once and forever. The incriminating paragraph was a quotation from a sermon by a nineteenth century preacher of the Transylvanian Enlightenment, Gergely Kozma.

> *Ministers should not limit themselves exclusively to the Bible in the choice of the theme of their sermons, but they should extend their sources of inspiration. One cannot be insensitive to the consequences of historical and natural catastrophes in the lives of the congregation (for example, pestilence, invasion of locusts, the revolt led by Horea, and other miseries).*

Considering the Transylvanian Unitarians' strict Biblical preaching at that time, Gergely Kozma's call had been quite a remarkable leap in liberal religious thinking. Imre's alleged political crime this time was putting *pestilence, locusts* and Romanian peasant leader *Horea* in the same phrase and calling them *miseries*. These were real events in Rev. Kozma's time and he, not Imre, had used them as examples. But quoting them a century later meant political suicide for Imre.

He was summoned to appear before government officials. They improvised a furious intimidation campaign and a kangaroo trial wherein the "prosecution" scandalized Imre and accused him of compromising the integrity and undermining the reputation of the Protestant Theological School. The attack was so unexpected and overpowering that Imre did not even try to defend himself. Under coercion he had to offer apologies to his Church and the state for "insulting the people of Romania." The "verdict" for that incriminating quotation was that Imre was to be immediately removed from the doctoral program, and the right to apply again was denied *forever.*

Finita est comedia! The character assassination by the secret police with the help of loyal collaborators in the Church meant a "final solution" concerning Imre. He had no legal defense nor anyone in the church to protect him. He became an outcast overnight.

Campaigns afterward were designed to make Imre feel responsible for the disaster. His "sin" was that he had brought state wrath upon the Church. His "feeble defense" was that he wanted to serve his church with his whole being and talent, to transfuse his accumulated knowledge and passion to the next generation of ministers. His aspirations were deemed incompatible with a church that fit more and more into the state system. Imre was left with a deep sense of guilt for having harmed his beloved church. His spirit broke this time and he never quite recovered.

In April, 1972, he wrote the following letter to then vice-Bishop János Erdö, his former professor and prisonmate.

Homoródszentmárton, April 20, 1972

Dear János,

Enclosed, please find a study I have just written for the *Christian Seed Sower*, "The Historical Evolution of Unitarian Baptism." It is a sample from a comprehensive work I am now writing, the "Unitarian Liturgy." The paper is handwritten because, unfortunately, I cannot afford a typewriter. I am also sending a few randomly picked sermons for publication, if you need them at

all. My *Seed Sower* file is growing all the time with articles
submitted for publication. I wish to ask you, in case you don't
intend to publish, to send my previous theological studies back to
me: "Homiletical Directions," "Guiding Principles," "Our First
Book of Communion Homilies," "Francis David" (in the series
"Our Great Preachers") and "Homiletical Disposition." I am
planning to gather my scattered theological essays into an edited
volume this coming summer. I am only a half-time farmer in the
collective this year, so I expect to have more time.[1]

Presently I am arranging my short novels and stories into
another volume. I have about seventy such novels, dealing with
themes of Church history and religious education. It would be a
great satisfaction for me to see them published. You would be the
first to receive a copy of it.[2]

My essay on "Axiological Christianity" is still unfinished
because of my lack of source material and time, but my interest in
experimental psychology in the context of religious psychology
and sociology has reawakened lately. I have even begun to adapt
some of the basic psychological tests to the socio-psychological
aspects of religion. Some of these studies are already finished.
The task is very exciting. It would be great to talk with you about
it.

I am in continuous battle with my many kinds of health
problems. My back pain and my kidney stones especially often
turn my life into misery. Yet I am in the midst of an unexpected
building project. A part of our parsonage simply collapsed and it
takes enormous energy and money to insure its safety. I myself

---

[1]Zizi was inspired by this letter to look for these writings. She gathered them
together, and learning about her father's plan for a new Liturgy book, she published
a volume of his essays and studies on practical theology. The Hungarian volumes
were distributed among ministers and students in Transylvania immediately after
the fall of Ceausescu to serve as a textbook in their studies of practical theology.

[2]They are lost. Some fifty pages of Rev. Gellérd's short novels and poems
had been in the possession of Rev. Dénes Szász of Székelyudvarhely for many
years. Zizi finally wanted them back. In a conversation by phone, she gave him
details of the time and place of her border crossing. Her phone conversation with
Rev. Szász was apparently intercepted by the secret police, for custom officers
were waiting for her at the border and confiscated all of Rev. Gellérd's writings.
They have never been returned.

work as a helping hand to the bricklayers, but my pig farm is a much bigger workload. Unfortunately, the additional income is indispensable to my meager salary. Twelve cute piglets are running around my backyard right now.

Thank you for the English Bible. I have no greater pleasure than reading it without a dictionary!

I had been in Kolozsvár recently and I wanted to visit you, but a deep sense of embarrassment prevented me from it. Yes, it was my doctoral dissertation and the scandal that it evoked. The judgment that I compromised the reputation of the Theological School turned our church and seminary officials against me. They treat me with resentment. I have become a *persona ingrata* in my own beloved Church. People are visibly afraid of me. My point is not that you, too, are afraid, but it is my duty to protect my colleagues from an undesired encounter with me.

I have requested the Theological School to send both my thesis and my dissertation back to me. Because they are considered compromising works, I hope for their return. I have requested the same from the Department of Cults in Bucharest.

My great concern now is that my writings might also be rejected by the *Christian Seed Sower*. I have already heard rumors that the journal is rather reluctant to publish my work any more. I am not angry; I understand the policy. But it hurts! Nobody in our church rejoiced at its resumed publication more than I did. What an irony of fate that I am the one banned from publishing in it, when I have been dreaming of it and writing for it all my life. I have so much to offer! Yet if you think that the *Seed Sower* is better off without my writings, don't push for them. My colleagues have advised me to ask for the publication of my work anonymously. I don't consider that right or ethical. I would rather give up. I can't help nurturing the hope, however, that sometime in the future, when the storm is over, my time will eventually come. Until such time I keep working quietly.

I know that I am expected to take this new tragedy of my life with good faith, like the failure in my graduate studies and the loss of my family and my beloved congregation. It is my fault that all these things happened to me; I don't blame or accuse anybody else.

I think of you often. I have flashbacks to the time spent with
you in the prison camps in the Danube Delta. In my depressing
loneliness I keep asking myself, wouldn't it have been better for
me to perish there, to rest in peace under the giant willow trees on
the banks of the Danube? This is much more than a passing mood
of depression. A deep inner fatigue has entered my life that was
unknown before. It is hard to accept it. I wish I were seventy and
could retire, but there is still much struggle and labor ahead.

Yours in faith, Imre

Ray of Light

There was much labor, but there was also some joy. It came with
his children. All the hard work and financial sacrifices to support Zizi in
her studies were indeed a blessing on the day of her graduation from medical
school in 1973. She graduated *summa cum laude,* ranking first in her class
of 260, and among the top nationally. Her excellence carried on the family
tradition. Judit and Imre were present during the solemn ceremony in the
grand hall of the Cultural Palace in Marosvásárhely when Zizi took the
Hippocratic Oath and received the Medical Doctor degree, the reward of
six years of hard work. Imre wrote her this letter on May 28, 1973:

Among those beautiful young doctors you were the shining
star, Zizi. I speak also for your mother when I say that your taking
the oath was the moment of our lives, the fulfillment of our aborted
dreams of becoming what you are today. Through your inauguration
I feel as if I too have became a physician.

I have been waiting for this moment more than anything. I
prayed to live to see this day. Now it will be easier to die. I say
with old Simeon:

"Lord, now let your servant depart in peace, for my eyes have
seen your salvation." Do you realize that you have accomplished
what both of your parents could only long for? I want to shout to
the world, "My daughter has become a Medical Doctor!"

Now I have one more wish left: to marry you off. Marriage
will be an even more decisive step in your life. I don't want to
influence you, but I have my own expectations. Your husband
should be similar to you but in a more balanced, quiet way. Like
you, he should love beauty and life but not eccentrically; succeed
but not at any price; be intelligent but not trivially; tune to the

modern trends but cultivate depth too; carry humanity in his spirit and readiness for action; and most of all, be understanding and loving, unconditionally loving. Oh, God, let me live to see your marriage!

You are, Zizi, the one whom I love the most in this world. Sometimes I even ask myself a bizarre question: whom do I love more, God or my daughter? I am not sure that in the'final analysis you would emerge the loser. This is a confession of a father, but it should never impose any obligation on you. Love must be liberating, not burdening or smothering.

Zizi's unannounced visits to her father brought sunshine to his dusky life. Her presence was an intense healing for him. He could sleep and regained his appetite and creative energy. She incited a sense of meaning and future.

The two of them wandered among the surrounding hills, their favorite hiding place from Imre's ever-needy parishioners. Zizi occasionally rebelled against the lack of privacy, and demanded this escape, if just for an hour. From the birch grove on the hilltop they looked down upon the beautiful village and lost themselves in exciting discussions about her studies, his writings, the books they read, the dreams they shared. They picked mushrooms and berries. Later Zizi took over his kitchen and prepared a fine dinner from the mushrooms. He brought his ruby-colored raspberry wine from the cellar. After dinner she played her violin and he accompanied her on the old piano. They were each other's appreciating audience. She sometimes appeared in his church unexpectedly, just minutes before he climbed the steps to the high pulpit, and he was lifted by joy and inspiration.

That autumn he traveled to Marosvásárhely for Zizi's first concert with the Medical Chamber Orchestra that she had founded in her Medical School. She was also its solo violinist, playing a Vivaldi concerto. In her long white dress she looked like an angel—her father's angel. The large audience, including her professors, colleagues, and even the regional Communist Party Secretary, celebrated her, the star of the evening, with a standing ovation. How he wished to share his tremendous joy with Judit, who was also present, but he declined Zizi's invitation to join them in the celebration afterwards and left alone in the dark night.

Daughter's Dilemma

Soon after Zizi's graduation, the only family doctor's position in her father's village became vacant and available to her. The medical office was in Homoródszentmárton and many surrounding villages belonged to it. Bad road conditions and the lack of adequate communication and transportation could turn emergencies, accidents and childbirth in those remote villages into a nightmare for the district doctor. Her father took for granted that Zizi would respond positively to this chance to move closer to him. "I know that this job is hard, but it is heroic," he argued. "You are capable of facing any challenge and being a winner. If you accepted the job, you could stay in the parsonage with me and save most of your salary. I would fix up the other room for you. We would be together, together!"

It was a most heartbreaking decision for Zizi to decline and let the opportunity pass. She sensed her father's deepening depression, mostly because of his loneliness. She knew too well that moving in with him would alleviate his misery. This was his only chance to be happy again and it was her duty to make this sacrifice. She felt infinitely selfish when she chose professional aspirations higher than being a village doctor. While 99% of her colleagues had no other option but a three-year-long rural practice, she had earned a privileged position. She had won the competition for a three-year internship at the university clinics, which was the direct road for medical specialization and an academic career. She struggled continuously to overcome through excellence the political discrimination of being a member of an ethnic minority, and she was reluctant to give up the shortcut toward a promising clinical career. She was too ambitious. Later Zizi would never fully overcome the guilt for spurning her father.

Final Marginalization

In 1977-78 Imre received one more theoretical chance to teach at the Seminary, as a substitute for his former student Rev. Árpád Szabó while he spent one year studying at Meadville/Lombard Theological School in the United States.

Imre considered the opportunity but was reluctant to apply for this temporary job. He would not cheapen himself, he decided. Attaining a full faculty chair was the only effective way to accomplish his vision and to create deep-lasting values. Yet, if, by *mirabile dictu*, the Bishop had asked him, he would have accepted his invitation despite all these objections. To be ready at any moment, Imre began studying day and night, especially at night because his parish surprised him with unexpected projects. Once, for example, he learned that the ceiling of his church was about to collapse, and he had to invest his time and energy into painstaking fundraising from his impecunious and parsimonious parishioners. His preparations, however, were all for nothing. Imre never received that invitation from the Bishop. There was no way, not even a narrow pathway, on which to break free from behind the walls of political exile which was growing into an inner exile.

He no longer went to General Assemblies of the Church. They were occasions when he would be cruelly reminded of his marginalization and a sense of being left behind. His broken life and career made him miserable. Church leaders performed, but Imre only listened. Happy families of ministers enjoyed the city while he longed for his lost family. General Assemblies lured him with the prospects of where he was supposed to be, and that was very painful. If the positions he deserved were denied to him, at least he tried to shield himself from seeing them.

In 1974 the pulpit of Kolozsvár once again became unexpectedly vacant. Imre couldn't help but allow his hopes to reawaken. Not for long though. During a two-day ministerial meeting at which members of the Headquarters and the state inspector were also present, Imre became a target of their malice and tactics of humiliation. Among others, he was reminded that he was old, short, and ugly—and he was willing to admit that they were right. The Headquarters' clear strategy was to discourage him from applying for the job in Kolozsvár and they accomplished their goal. It might sound like sour grapes, but Imre finally realized the sad truth, that the atmosphere at the Unitarian Headquarters of animosity, jealousy, and discord made cooperation and productive work for his Church virtually impossible.

His congregation's indolence and his loneliness created a suffocating wall around Imre. The congregation promised to raise his salary and build a bathroom, but he knew too well that they couldn't afford it. In fact, he had heard rumors that some of his parishioners rebelled against an official notice from the Headquarters that ordered them to raise their minister's salary. He spent most of his professional career making his living by farming. Not that he didn't like to farm, but he felt that he was wasting his life with it. He should focus on the creative work for which he was trained and which only he could do: writing, teaching, raising a future generation of ministers instead of pigs. There was still enough vitality in him to recognize that he had to move away from this village. If not for other reasons, he had to create social opportunities to meet new people—someone special, perhaps.

Siménfalva, the embodiment of happiness, was Imre's place to take an occasional pilgrimage to heal. Siménfalva was also a place of grief, the lost paradise. The urge to blossom once more was still within him. Judit's love still haunted him. His earnest attempt to reconcile their marriage had failed, and her rejection was final. Every time he visited his son, he had to go through the aggravation of her open aversion. He always went packed with village delicacies and he supported his children beyond what he could comfortably afford. He would have given his life for Judit. He still loved her; she was the only women he ever loved. This stubborn love had become a wall of inhibition toward other women. Imre's obsession with Judit, he feared, made him unfit for a new marriage. A lady friend in Kolozsvár showed interest in marrying Imre, but only if he moved to Kolozsvár. She would not give up her city culture and comfort for the misery of the village.

A Mere Epilogue

A move to a different church also became necessary for Imre professionally. Just as he was gathering strength for a change, a ministry in Torda, the historic city in the neighborhood of Kolozsv·r, became vacant. The congregation asked him to candidate, and he was scheduled to preach on a designated Sunday. The telegram of their notice, however, arrived the Monday after that Sunday, and he lost this chance. The other candidate, the Bishop's choice, won the contest by preaching an Imre Gellérd sermon!

The next vacant pulpit was in Sepsiszentgyörgy, a large city and a cultural center of the Hungarian minority. Good job opportunities and a friendly city administration attracted people from the economically strangled villages of the Háromszék region. More than 3,000 Unitarians ended up in this city which did not have a Unitarian church, only a small meeting house. The congregation, yet to be organized, had a large number of educated people, doctors, teachers, engineers and young families with children. They wanted to build a church, and unanimously invited Imre to become their minister. A delegation visited his parish and were reluctant to leave unless he said yes. He promised to think about it, and they promised to come back the next day for his answer. What a dreadful night! Zizi somehow found this out and appeared with an agenda. They were up all night arguing, for she passionately insisted that her father accept the invitation. "I am too old," he argued, "I would surely die of heart attack. There would be too much stress involved in building a new congregation

and a new church." Zizi counter-argued, "There are great doctors and
hospitals in the city, so you would be much safer there with your heart
condition. You would have an intellectually challenging congregation, a
good social life, the theater and library. Your talent would be appreciated
and put to worthy use. The city needs you. A new and challenging life
would cure your depression. Marking time in a dead place eventually results
in the death of the spirit." The next day Imre could not say *yes*. He simply
did not have the inner strength.

His reluctance stirred an avalanche of anger in the Unitarian
Headquarters. The leaders in Kolozsvár had held their breath: "Will the
Imre Gellérd problem ever go away?" Imre weighed too heavily on their
conscience and he was expected to accept compromises, but he stubbornly
resisted. His place was among the theological school's faculty. He knew it;
they knew it. The students needed him there. Why should he make
compromises against the interest of his church and himself in order to
assuage the guilt of the leaders? His ministry in a village was dignifying
enough. He didn't want just a career for the sake of it. He would only
accept a position in the Theological School, nothing else, nothing less. He
was not interested in half solutions. He owed this much to his own dignity.

Besides, he dreaded change all his life, and changing congregations
was the worst kind of change. To start everything from scratch, to make all
the adjustments that a ministry required, to get to know so many new people
and try to untangle their lives, to try to please everybody. He didn't feel
that he had enough energy for that. In a new congregation there is no past,
no cumulated energies, and he was tired of proving himself over and over
again. "Why try to fool a new community?" he used another argument. "I
have a strong premonition of the impending end of my life. I would rather
stay in Homoródszentmárton. With my broken life I feel strongly about
staying close to the home of my mother and brothers. This is a much greater
power than inertia."

Sepsiszentgyörgy finally invited Rev. Áron Török, Imre's former
student, a great talent of the church, and his close friend. After his installation
in 1973, Imre congratulated him:

Dear Áron,
I apologize for not participating in your installation ceremonies,
but I stay away from large church events. I have already heard
odes about your energetic leadership. You are the one whom the

church of Sepsiszentgyörgy really needed! I praise God that it happened in this way. We are all proud of you and wish you success. I don't expect you to write me, just remember me sometimes. My life has entered into the vale of twilight. All my creative work is now a mere epilogue. Nobody needs me any more. Neither do I need others. There is a single star still shining in my life: Zizi. She has just graduated from Medical School and is writing her final thesis now. May I ask you to congratulate her. It would make her so happy.

Religious life of the Homoród valley slumbers. Small wakenings, occasional kindlings are insufficient for a shake-up. It takes God's mighty power to shock these villages into life. The churches of the Nyikó valley are also sleeping. And who knows, will they ever wake up again?

Keep our people alive,

Áron! Don't lose heart when the seeds you sow fall on barren ground. Some will bring fruit. I see myself in you, my heroic self, that of the Siménfalva years. Your successes remind me of what I have been but never can be again. How sad when the candle is blown out! But you should shine. Be the messenger for the people of Háromszék.

P.S. I am not sure whether we will meet again, so I wish to make a confession now. I want to express my long due and sincere gratitude—my tears flow when I just think of it—that you confirmed Zizi in the Unitarian faith, and by doing it, you decisively helped her stay loyal to me and stand by me. Thank you, that you filled her spirit with faith and supported her in many ways. May God richly bless you, dear Friend!

To lighten the burden of my huge sense of indebtedness toward you, I wish to tell you something that you might not be aware of. In the prison I too suffered for you. With my suffering I was able to prevent you from receiving the same fate as mine. You see, we were exchanging sacrifices. Thank you for yours! Imre.

* * *

Imre's never stopped writing his sermons and giving his pearls by the dozen to his colleagues who asked for them by the dozen. He never judged their talent less; he hoped for a form of redemption through this recognition.

CHAPTER 10

Parenting

I n the inventory of losses caused by Imre's imprisonment, the loss of his son to Roman Catholicism was a very sensitive one. Andor was his sacred task, he reasoned, so he invested his hopes in him. By the time they finally reunited after prison, Imre was a stranger to Andor. His loyalty exclusively belonged to his mother. It was not that Andor didn't show curiosity for his father's reappearance and prison stories, but Imre did not sense the love of the son toward his father. Andor seemed to be conditioned to having only one parent. What concerned Imre more was his own inability to accept his son unconditionally. He viewed Andor's conversion as part of Judit's punishment toward him. She now controlled Andor's life in all its fullness. She perceived Imre, the Unitarian minister father, to be a certain threat in *her* son's religious life. Andor had become the prize of two competing parents. Religion was too important to both of them, and their son's identity was a matter of their own power struggle under the mask of religion. Judit had taken the show trial at its face value, and she accused him of "allowing" himself to be imprisoned. She had a way of trivializing Imre's suffering for his convictions.

Imre was unwilling to accept his son's continued upbringing by Roman Catholic priests. His parental and professional pride was insulted by Andor's God-father being a priest and his God-mother a nun. The historical hostility between Unitarians and Roman Catholics, the persecuted and the persecutor, grew into an existential animosity in Imre toward the Catholic clergy. How could this be? He had not only lived with them in prison, but there he loved them as his friends.

Imre hoped, as any father would, to do projects with his son, to make him interested in literature and his father's writings, to have conversations with him about life and spiritual matters. Yet he found himself withdrawn by his own resentment for the betrayal of their shared faith. Zizi tried to play the catalyst in their coming together, but she laid guilt on her brother, which did not produce any good results. With all his pedagogical and psychological training, Imre was unable to break down their separation.

Then, one glorious day in 1978, the prodigal son returned to the arms of his father. The morning star appeared in the horizon of his lonesome life. It came about during a conversation while hiking in the forest. Andor had fallen in love, and with it came certain confusion. He needed a male viewpoint toward understanding his dilemmas. It was this moment when he suddenly glimpsed his father's very similar anguish. Imre was captivated by the discovery of Andor's pure and transparent soul and compelling personality. In that autumn afternoon they discovered each other's vulnerability—and humanity. That brought about the will to clear away the grudges away from the way of their relationship. Imre had to overcome his resentment for his son's disloyalty, and Andor, his guilt. Father and son, man to man, were trying to find their authentic roles in each other's context. They had to fundamentally redefine themselves in this new relationship. They tried out the traditional male roles, but they were utterly awkward in them.

All the miseries of Imre's life became subordinated to his new relationship. Andor visited him almost daily on his motorcycle. He now sought Imre's advice, not just his financial support. He introduced his new girlfriend to him. They engaged in profound discussions. Imre found himself eagerly waiting for their visits that always renewed his spirit. Like in his dreams they now did things together—hoeing the corn during spring and harvesting the fruit of their shared labor during the fall. Andor cut wood for him and helped pick apples and harvest grapes. They pressed the cider and watched day by day how it fermented into wine, their wine! Theirs was a relationship of quiet every-days, which Imre could never have had with the soaring, restless Zizi.

To his great surprise and considerable pride, Andor electrically re-wired the entire parsonage and repaired just about everything in and around the house. He was a true specialist in the technical aspects of life for which Imre had little dexterity. After years of lamentation he wrote to Zizi: "Imagine, Andorka and I, father and son alongside, are working together for the same goal!"

Simple Serenity

The gift of his son came in time to console him in an expected but never easily accepted loss, his mother's death. She was ninety years old in 1978 when she died, a widow for fifty years. Fearlessly independent and non-conforming, Julianna embarrassed her Transylvanian lesser nobility family of a few times. She ended up poor but happy because her five children were happy around her.

By coerced match-making she married a rich young man whom she did not love and whom she left soon after. She secretly nurtured a passionate love for a man, the father of her daughter Julianna. She never revealed her lover's name. For a few years she had been the housekeeper of a renowned Unitarian minister-poet in Kénos, but her family disapproved of her unconventional lifestyle and nagged her to marry a much older man. She at first was reluctant to conceive, but soon got pregnant with Imre, then in a short succession with two more sons, Ferenc and Albert. Her husband died seven years later and the thirty-nine year-old widow was left with four small children. A few years later she re-married and gave birth to another boy Dénes. But this husband was an alcoholic, so she sent him away.

Theirs was a happy home; hers was uncomplicated love. She was a master storyteller, with great humor and a healthy life philosophy. Though uneducated she had an amazing ability to guide her children with her down-to-earth wisdom. She truly embodied a religious symbol, the pelican, which feeds its offspring from its own mouth. It was utterly healing to be surrounded by her simple serenity.

In her old age, practically blind, she was always waiting for Imre and Zizi, but showed genuine surprise when they occasionally showed up at Julianna's home where the two of them lived. Their only room, always tidy, was filled with laughter. Nothing made her happier than being examined by her doctor granddaughter. She swore that Zizi's medical check cured her of whatever illness she might have had.

Imre was his mother's favorite. It was her wish that he become a Unitarian minister. Deeply religious though unorthodox, she prayed throughout her life and especially during her son's prison years. When Imre came home from jail, she gave him a Bible at a time Bibles were a forbidden and practically unobtainable treasure. Imre was not ready to let her go.

On a cold January night their family gathered around her flower-covered catafalque for the last vigil. As was traditional, the vigil lasted for the entire night before the funeral. Friends and neighbors spent the night together telling stories of the deceased, praying and singing hymns. Imre thought that there was light around her even in death.

Hostile Borders, Fake Marriage

Andor's return to his father meant consolation for yet another trauma, Zizi's departure from the country in the summer of 1978. Zizi was going to marry a man who lived in Hungary. She was prepared to leave behind everything she had painstakingly built in her medical career, and immigrate to Hungary, a neighboring Communist country. Imre could not follow her furious pace. He was hardly ever able to leave his village, his attachment was so strong. She was everything her parents wanted to be and she remained loyal to his values, yet Imre had such different dreams for her future.

He begged her, "Don't go, my Zizi, don't waste your talent in a foreign land. It is much needed here at home in Transylvania!" He worried about her endeavor, the grand adventure of a pretended marriage to escape Romania, and he hoped that she would find a true husband. She was already thirty! He acknowledged to himself that he was old and represented different values that were perhaps anachronistic. She was the joy of his life, but she gave him an equal dose of anxiety. What he was imagining for her were simple things, a conventional happiness that included home, family, children, car, money and summer vacations at his parish. He knew that such things would lead to an ordinary life, but he believed that one must accept life's confining routines. He was afraid that Zizi would be lost, overcome, defeated and left behind by sophisticated people of the great metropolis Budapest. He warned her, "It is easier to be outstanding here at home. It is easier to shine when others around us mirror back your own glow. To shine even when the light is being absorbed by blackened mirrors—that is your challenge!"

Imre had offered to buy Zizi an apartment in Marosvásárhely, but she didn't value material well-being or stability. She was strong-willed and had set the immigration process into motion. Soon hostile national borders would separate them from each other, for their Hungarian motherland was also Romania's official enemy. Imre sent her forward with his prayers that she would not be sorry for her daring move. "If disappointment disheartens you, my daughter, you know that you always have a home here. I hope I will be here to comfort you."

Zizi's weekly letters from Budapest brought anything but disappointment. She amazed her father with her fearless ambition and luck. She achieved more in a few weeks than others did in years, if at all. While Imre celebrated her successes, he also grieved again over losing her. His letters to her were the antitheses of her optimism; he could not hide his depression from her. He would soon be sixty and he dreaded the thought of aging. One who was sixty was old, they both thought. And he was alone, alone again, and just marking time. He was afraid that his depression would eventually kill him. He contemplated retirement, not that it would solve anything. In fact ministers' greatest anxiety was retirement because they would have to move out of the parsonage, and many such as Imre had no place to go. Hence, ministers wanted to serve until old age or until their death. Dying in the pulpit was a final glory.

Since Zizi had declined her father's offer to buy an apartment, he decided to buy one for his own retirement in Székelyudvarhely, where his siblings and his son lived. By the time he made up his mind, his savings had shrunk because of inflation and rapidly escalating prices, and he had to save more money. When the right amount was finally together, he learned that he had no right to purchase estates in the city because he was not a resident there. They eventually found a loophole. Andor used his privileges through his workplace to sign up for an apartment in his name. The downside was, the apartment was on the fifth floor with no elevator. Andor was young and considered capable of climbing the stairs, and to accommodate his father was dangerous because that might have revealed the scheme. Thus, Imre was stuck with moving to an expensive apartment with the anxiety that he would not be able to climb the stairs as he became older. Moreover, the apartment was miserable and in a depressing environment. The narrow streets left no space between the gray concrete cages. Ceausescu's obsession to save farmland translated into impossibly narrow streets. People could look into each other's bedrooms. Noise from children playing in the dusty streets reverberated in the walls. The walls had not been insulated properly in the first place and the hundreds of TV and radio programs turned this into a cacophony, amplified by the canyon of concrete walls. People from neighboring villages, from traditional communities, who moved into the city to find jobs were trapped in this cement jungle.

Andor and Zizi tried to make their father's future home—or rather a dungeon—a happy place for retirement. They furnished it with Zizi's collection of village antiques, nineteenth century peasant painted furniture. But Imre just could not imagine himself living in that place. It promised total isolation. The window overlooking the cemetery was the only comfort. In ordinary circumstances he would gladly exchange the apartment for one at Zizi's place, but Zizi was now a foreign citizen.

Before long Zizi revealed her principle reason for changing countries. With his days wasting away in the village and his career at a dead end in Transylvania, she tried to create conditions and find solutions for him as much as for herself in the new country. In spite of his firm refusal ever to move to Hungary, she still hoped that retirement eventually would change his mind.

They both were aware there were vacant parishes in Hungary, but they avoided talking about the issue. As soon as she arrived in Budapest, she paid a visit to Dr. József Ferencz, Bishop of the Hungarian Unitarian Church. The Bishop welcomed her but knew why she had come. He opened the conversation with, "There is no job in our church for your father. You'd better know it in case you might have hopes. Your father is too 'complicated' and we want simple ministers here." In the following years his point was proven. His church was not a church for Imre nor for Zizi.[1]

The Departing Train

In the summer of 1979, after much persuasion, Imre finally visited his daughter in Budapest for three weeks. This was his first vacation in fifteen years. To get a passport, his first, was a dreaded ordeal for him. He had to deal with secret police agents and be exposed to hostile interrogations which triggered prison memories. Eventually the passport was granted but he still procrastinated about his visit, since someone always needed him in the village. Then one day the Rev. Sándor Zoltán, Imre's predecessor, suddenly died in Budapest, and he had expressed the desire to be buried by Rev. Gellérd. Now he had to leave. He arrived in Budapest very ill, with shivers and high fever. He collapsed upon arrival, and Zizi rushed him to her hospital. He had a massive, purulent infection of his gums and sinuses. Because intense headaches had long tormented him, he kept increasing the doses of aspirin until his condition became critical. Thus, Rev. Zoltán's death was a life-saving gift to Imre. The other "favor" from his colleague was Imre's only chance to preach in Budapest and bury his friend's urn under a shovelful of earth brought from their shared village Homoródszentmárton.

The three weeks spent in Zizi's tiny flat were their happiest and longest time together. For the first time in his adult life, Imre was able to listen to the Hungarian National Anthem sung by Zizi's choir in the Roman

---

[1] The small Hungarian Unitarian Church was forged from a district of the Transylvanian Unitarian Church that lay within Communist Hungary's borders. Most churches were able to protect their traditions from capitulating to the totalitarian regime. The Bishop of the Hungarian Unitarian Church, however, worked for the interest of the state.

Catholic Matthias Cathedral. Not just listen, but sing along openly! Many of his prisonmates received their sentences for allegedly listening to this Hungarian prayer on the radio. Imre first froze in fear, but then with tears flowing down his cheeks, he began to sing the words.

> God, bless the Hungarians,
> with joy and plenty.
> Shield them from harm
> When they fight their enemies.
> Bring years of happiness
> after torments for so long.
> This people has atoned
> its past and its future.

On July 30, 1979, Imre boarded the Orient Express at Budapest's West Station. As always, the train was overbooked, crowded, hot and miserable. Zizi had begged him to stay a little longer, but in a near-panic he had to leave at any cost! He recited many reasons that his congregation could not manage without him. Zizi ran off to buy him water and a snack for the long journey, but she returned a minute too late and could only see the receding rear of the train. The suddenness of their separation and her regret of not saying good-bye grew into a disproportionate sense of grief and the departing train, a recurring nightmare.

The time in Budapest rejuvenated Imre. With great surprise he finally felt comfortable in the metropolis. Every moment was meaningful and memorable. Zizi intuited his needs to be healed and be uplifted. She helped him discover what he needed to build into his life to face aging in dignity. He tapped into new sources of joy, which granted him renewed ambitions to work. He watched Zizi work in the largest hospital of the city, where ambulances arrived one after another, delivering patients to the physician on duty—Dr. Judit Gellérd, his daughter, his Zizi! He relished her success, a privileged position which was important, indispensable, where life and death met. He wrote to Zizi:

> Now I am not only able to identify with your professional life, Zizi, but I have realized the vicarious ways God operates. You are fulfilling the dreams of my youth, after all. I only need to have the perspective of timelessness. I had been like you, enthusiastic and open. Experiences touched me prolifically, but I was never able to

reach their harvest. Something always trampled my ears of corn. Now, finally, I rejoice at how God continues building my life in yours. What I admire in you is not your boundless energy, but your gift of intuition. You sense the right direction and have the courage to take the risk of diving into the swirl for the foreseen treasures. Hold on to this precious seismograph of your soul, and don't let rationality break it! It is my overriding rationality that leads to excessive fear from the unknown. I ponder the risks and benefits over and over, and somehow I always end up making the wrong choices. I can only count on the fact that I am never *Fortuna*'s favorite. It is hard to believe that one can be so favored by life, so consistently lifted to the peaks as you are, Zizi. Well, you have to achieve for both of us. It is quite possible that with the blessings in your life, God is making up for all the good things he "forgot" to provide us. The more God is giving you, the more I realize how much he had intended for me. This is true even if one considers luck as a human quality. "Talent is but the courage to start over again," Arthur Honegger said.

I must admit that I had prayed for a divine intervention that would have stopped you from emigrating. I am now grateful that those prayers were not answered either, a reminder that God's thoughts are not our thoughts.

So now I pray, "*Thank you, Lord, for the rising star of my daughter's life. Save her from becoming a comet which suddenly falls. If she is to suffer, let me take her sufferings on me. If that ever has to happen, I offer myself as a sacrifice for her. Keep her safe and bring her to the forefront of humanity.*"

CHAPTER 11

New Threats

I mre received an anonymous phone that he would soon be arrested again. The Securitate had approached his colleague in the next village to inform on Imre and denounce him, but he had the guts to say *No* to them. He would not betray his mentor. He rushed to Imre under cover of night to warn him about the impending danger. He begged Imre to give up tutoring students in his congregation, for state officials viewed his successful private program as an offense against society by a politically branded "class enemy." He also warned his friend to keep away from a certain meeting where he would be provoked and possibly arrested. Then he apologized for having to disappear from Imre's life; he was under surveillance, and his family would be in danger.

Fear set foot in Imre's bones once again. He could not abandon his students who needed his help. Poor education in the village school put these children at a tremendous disadvantage in university entrance exams. After a year of intense tutoring in just about every subject, his students made it into universities with few exceptions. He had received intimidating warnings about his "poisonous" influence on the youth before, but this was the first real threat of a new arrest. He would tolerate hunger, thirst and cold, but fear was intolerable.

A recent confrontation with state authorities suddenly gained new significance in this impending threat. It happened during one of the district ministers' meetings. He had been long waiting for a permit to refurbish his congregation's meeting hall, with no answer from Comrade Boga, the district Inspector of Religion. He held total power over church endeavors, from the simplest church celebration to the religious education curriculum and building projects. Imre humbly but persistently questioned Inspector Boga about the overdue permit until he turned into a raging beast and started screaming curses in denigrating language at his defenseless victim. This triggered all the memories and humiliation of prison, and Imre lost his composure. He began to shake uncontrollably and tried to escape from the room like a trapped animal. He ran directly into the glass window and broke it. He hit his head so hard that he fell to the floor, unconscious. There was a deadly silence in the room, he was later told. Intimidation surrounding the incident was pervasive. Representatives of the Headquarters said not one word of apology afterward, and nobody else dared to take up Imre's defense.

Inspector Boga was very satisfied with Imre's subjugation. Imre had been at his mercy to get a passport to Hungary, and he had tried to behave here in order to earn "good marks." But despite that confrontation with Comrade Boga, Imre resisted his intimidation tactics and continued to exercise his prerogatives in education. Not long after that incident, he held two sets of lectures, one with political content. He continued his work to enrich Unitarian heritage and educate his younger colleagues. When Headquarters asked for an annual report of ministers' work, Imre wrote and sent them a one-hundred-page theological-sociological study.

Wings With No Space to Fly

Writing was a compelling force for Imre. It was his way of being alive, overcoming hindrances. In his writing he wrestled with God. He wrote a poem after having a mystical experience in the mountains of the Southern Carpathians. He wrote to Zizi, "On the mountain peak of Cozia I had a flash of insight into the depth of truth. It was God's burning kiss on my forehead of creative desire and inspiration." His poem summarized all the ambiguities of his human condition and his wrestling with the Creator.

"Lord, I don't ask for freedom if you grant me space.
I find peace, finally, in my cage."
Winged prisoner, languishing among narrow walls,
Thus beseeching the silent sky.

And the cage expanded. Winged prisoner greedily breathed
The sweet nectar of a new realm.
And suddenly, through iron bars,
He glimpsed the snow peak, close and fascinating.

"Lord, this new home is still too narrow,
Let me build dream castles under the stars."
"You may not," said the Messenger,"'this is your place."
"No? Then, Lord, take my useless wings away."

"Lord, you've done shoddy work in me,
Giving me wings but no space to fly.

Let the harmony be re-established,
Take my talents back from me!"

And the Messenger said:
"Keep them and learn: high soaring is not always the key to
     glory,
But the pure effort of small, fluttering strokes.
Neither is iron molded by power hammers,
Rather by continuous, precise, tiny blows.

"I know that creeping humiliates you
And the grace of height excites your wings.
But calm down: depth can be a peak, too,
And the crest sometimes witnesses vain soaring.

"The valley is not where you long for flight
And is not the peak where vain peacocks try to dazzle the sun.
Soulless spirits lower the mountains into valleys
And summit-hearts elevate tomorrows into heights.

"Crawling with broken wings you still can lead,
Or one can mark time in boots of seven leagues.
Because it is not the size of wings and plans that matters,
But something else: after knowing all of this,
Do you really wish to fly to the illusory peaks?"

"I must admit, I did wish. Don't blackmail me, Lord, with that
'illusory' attribute. However, Thy will be done...yet forgive my rebellion,"
Imre pleaded.

The writing impulse can be revelatory. Imre found himself writing
in his new 1980 calendar the following prophecy in French: *"L'année du
mon mort....Je ne crois pus que je puisse remplir ce cahier"* ["The year of
my death. I don't think I will be able to fill this notebook"]. After this slip
happened, he began to contemplate its reality. Soon he wrote in his notebook
a strange funeral text, *his* funeral text, borrowing from the great poet Endre
Ady: *"Ash-covered ruins of long extinct fires...."*

Imre remembered that Zizi had sung Mozart's *Requiem* in her
church, dedicating it to her grandmother's memory. A great desire rose in
Imre to be buried with this*Requiem* sung. He asked her to bring him a
recording of it.

The thought that Zizi would be home by Christmas made Imre increasingly nervous. "How can I shield my thoughts from her? Or should I? I managed to diffuse her suspicion at her last visit...." At that last visit he had insisted that Zizi come with him to visit their relatives in Kénos. They had never done that before. He took her from house to house, for he was related to almost every family in one way or another. Their visit stirred such excitement in the village that they couldn't leave anybody out. On that afternoon they reconstructed their family tree and its saga. Many real and imaginary stories were told of family exploits. Imre was proud of his kinfolk and proud of his daughter. A vacuum in their relationship was finally filled with a strong sense of coherence.

At Kénos something Imre had done left Zizi speechless. She might not have approved had he asked her beforehand. What he did was introduce her as a married woman. She was married, after all. Although she always insisted that her marriage was merely a *pro forma* arrangement to escape Romania, Imre wanted to believe, if just for one hour, that she would continue the line of their family, that she would bear children. Besides, he very much liked her pseudo-husband, an artist, a monumental sculptor from Hungary. Imre couldn't have imagined a more suitable husband for Zizi. He was gentle and intelligent, handsome and talented, yet Zizi insisted that theirs would not be a matrimonial relationship. Of course, she could not contradict him in Kénos because the pretended marriage had to be kept an absolute secret. She had to play her role credibly, and her father so enjoyed the play! He hoped to precipitate some reconsideration of her stubborn resistance.

Imre knew what the "problem" with Zizi was. She was in love with a prominent composer, her former music professor. If they were to be together, Zizi would have to move back to Transylvania. That gave Imre new hopes for having her daughter back, but reversing her immigration boggled his mind. Her previous emigration from Romania took four years of waiting. She was also without any citizenship for a few months. The reversal seemed a daunting task, but Zizi was prepared to plunge ahead with it. She and the composer had visited Imre last August, bringing along his son. Imre had stage fever before meeting him, one of the admired men of their country, but their encounter was profound. He promised to visit Imre as often as he could. They even set a tentative time of their next meeting, on Imre's sixtieth birthday.

Christmas

The last week of Advent in a village has a tangible sense of anticipation of the high holidays. It is the time of spiritual preparation for the Lord's Supper, a time when one is expected to straighten out one's troubled relationships with one's family, neighbors, and ultimately, God. This is a time of reflection on one's values and weaknesses. It is a time that creates the spiritual conditions for repentance and change, for asking and granting forgiveness. The Lord's Supper is ideally the culmination and the sacred moment of being face to face with one's conscience and highest values, an intense moment of communion with the divine and the neighbor. In that hour Jesus symbolically invites his people to sit at the table and eat and drink, to absorb the higher values of spiritual transformation so that they can prepare similar tables for others.

For Unitarians the communion is merely the starting point in the process of growth. It is the first step on the path toward the transcendent. It is the divine spark which starts positive changes, and it is the fuse which leads to correct actions. It is a stepping stone, not an escalator. It won't bring automatic salvation. One has to walk on the path, making personal efforts, taking personal responsibility. The preparations for the Lord's Supper also have a capacity for personal growth, as great as the ritual itself.

* * *

It was Advent in Homoródszentmárton, the time of preparation.

As he had done for the past several years, Andor asked his father to host him and his friends for their New Year's party in the parsonage. His father's unexpected refusal of his request stunned Andor. The reason given was even stranger; he had already convoked a reunion of his former prisonmates, he informed his son, while feeling terribly guilty for lying.

He hoped that both of his children would nevertheless spend the Christmas with him. On the Holy Night he decorated a beautiful Christmas tree, cooked their favorite dinner, put the best wine on the table, and waited. He expected Zizi's arrival from Budapest that day, but one could never know when border guards and custom officers would harass travelers. Last Easter, for example, she was pulled off the train in the middle of the night, guarded by armed soldiers all night and sent back to Budapest the next morning because she tried to'"smuggle" in a book and medicine for her father. She was put on the black list at that border point. She came home anyway, crossing the border at a different place and walking the last seventeen kilometers to her father's village, to be at church for the Lord's Supper.

It was almost midnight. The candles burned down, the dinner got cold, and he never felt so alone as a father. Suddenly, like an angel, Zizi burst into his solitude. Andor was not with her. Any holiday was a time of hard choices for children who felt torn by conflicting loyalties toward their divorced parents, and Andor had to attend the Catholic mass with his mother. Zizi made a deal with her, splitting her Christmas Eve between them. She caught the last commuter bus and surprised him. Zizi was not her usual happy, bubbly self. She was grieving over her unexpected breakup with her composer friend. Her pain reverberated in Imre. He held her and comforted her. He knew that this would also take away any reason for re-immigrating to Transylvania.

Her sadness did not ruin their Christmas joy. Zizi presented a big surprise for him, a taperecorder, a rarity at that time. It came with a string attached: Zizi wanted her father to record his sermons. They immediately recorded their own singing of the entire repertoire of their favorite songs, many of them of his own composition. Then they listened to their voices as Zizi's high soprano harmonized with her father's tenor. "Your voice sounds like crystal bells, pure and warm. You have the voice of angels, do you know, Zizi?" This was a prized "discovery" to her since she had never thought of herself as a singer before. Two loving spirits embraced that memorable evening, and that was bliss for them.

Imre's Christmas service showcased his oratorial talent. The sermon, "Behold, I Bring You Great Joy," was a homiletical masterpiece, a summary of his personal theology about the immanence of salvation. It was the sheer essence of Unitarianism. The culminating moment of the service was the Lord's Supper. "This is my body.... This is my blood...." His face lit up with holiness as he lifted up the chalice. "Do this in memory of me!" An inner light hid the scars of all his suffering. Zizi remembered, "As I took the homemade bread and the chalice from my father's callused hands, we looked into each other's eyes. I trembled in the power of the moment. It was 'trans-substantiation' for me; my spiritual substance, my very core was transformed."

She recorded her father's sermon so that he could listen to his own voice for the first time. He was thrilled when she replayed it for him, and he promised to record each of his future sermons. "From now on I will be preaching to you, so I won't be discouraged if the church is ever empty."

No Good-Bye

Christmas of 1979 was clear day, beautifully white from a recent snowstorm. Zizi loved to walk with her father to the neighboring village of Lókod, his second congregation, for the afternoon worship service. Holding each other arm in arm, they ploughed a furrow in the glittering virgin snow, the entwining footsteps of two children of God.

Zizi left him the next day to go back to her mother's, since both her parents needed their children's healing presence. Imre visited her there every day. He hoped that he might meet his son also, but Andor came home from his factory job about the same time as his mother did, and Imre did not want to face Judit's coldness. Despite everything he was still attracted to her.

Zizi had to leave on New Year's day for hospital duty in Budapest. Imre came to say good-bye and was lucky this time. His son came home early and they could finally have a beer together, their favorite ritual. Judit joined them in unusually good spirits.

Imre could not bear the intensity of the *farewell*, so he summarily decided he had to leave and fled. Zizi ran after him, pleading with him to stay longer. She reproached him that his congregation was his only priority, and they never had enough time together. "Please, Daddy, stay just until the last bus! I want to talk to you about, about life," she tried to blackmail him. His face quivered with distress and then she felt remorse. After all, she was the one who was leaving, always leaving him alone.

The last bus was overbooked. Imre panicked. He begged the clerk, a former student of his, to grant him a ticket. As if it were a matter of life and death, he forcibly squeezed himself into the overcrowded bus that was about to pull out of the station. He did not have time to kiss his daughter good-bye!

That last glimpse of his face distorted by pain haunted Zizi. Her father's eyes caught hers for a second, and she suddenly knew that something would happen. She did not have time to consider fully her premonition. She had to leave that evening; her hospital duty, seven hundred kilometers away, started the next day.

Blood on Red Carnation

That next day was New Year's Eve. Imre's heart was heavy with dark anticipation, yet he was completely unprepared for what would happen that day.

For fifteen years he had been taking his lunch at his next door neighbor's, the Soós family. At the beginning this was convenient, for he did not have an equipped kitchen nor time to cook for himself. Soon it turned into a terrible burden. The wife Ilona was a pathetic woman who became obsessed with spying on him. She harassed him and tried to control his life. She found new ways each day to try to make herself indispensable. Since her husband had been the church's lay president at the beginning of his ministry, there was no way he could free himself from her tyranny. He decided to ignore her, dealing with the situation as passively as possible.

The family needed his help more than he did theirs. Their oldest son suffered from schizophrenia and the youngest was mentally retarded and extremely impulsive. The father was a wreck of tuberculosis and arteriosclerosis. It was Imre's volunteered task to take him to Bucharest's tuberculosis hospital every time he needed treatment. Imre also made sure that their schizophrenic, older son received proper medical attention; otherwise, he turned violent, especially toward his mother. For more than a decade Imre tutored the youngest son daily, using all his pedagogical skills to push him through high school. The young man got a decent job and got married. Imre had invested tremendous amounts of time and energy into this wrecked family, but he had been unable to recapture his independence and privacy.

New Year's Eve was a very different day from all the others in a Transylvanian village. People stopped working and were in a casual mood. Men started their drinking parties in the morning to be properly tuned by midnight, when they said good-bye to the old year. This was a day of reckoning, a day of gift giving. Imre took his end-of-the-month lunch payment to his neighbor along with a bouquet of his home grown red carnations and a kerchief.

While Imre was eating lunch quietly, a roaring beast stormed into the kitchen. Drunken, with bloodshot eyes, the younger son screamed at the top of his voice, "So, they were right. The minister is molesting my mother!" He threw himself violently at the unsuspecting Imre. The scene was so bizarre Imre recoiled in horror. The man grabbed the large kitchen knife from the table and kept bellowing, "I'll kill the minister, I'll kill him!" and he began to chase him around the table with the knife. His mother, stepping into the kitchen at this moment, began to scream hysterically. It was an insane scene.

A primitive instinct of survival helped Imre pull himself out of the grasp of this mad giant, and almost miraculously he escaped through the door. His attacker jumped after him with such violence that he broke the glass panel of the doorway. The broken glass cut his leg and must have sliced the artery, for blood was gushing out like an artesian well. It seemed he would bleed to death, and Imre started to help him. His mother fortunately realized what happened and applied a compression on his injury. The bleeding stopped, but not his threats. "I will kill the minister! He won't escape from me, I'll find him, I'll kill him!" Imre fled and locked himself in the parsonage but he could still hear his former pupil's inarticulate screams from the ambulance as they rushed him to the hospital.

Imre was in shock. He had been attacked at the minister's meeting by Comrade Boga, he had received the "courtesy warning" of his impending arrest, and now he was attacked in his own village. He was to be accused of crimes against the state, and now he was being accused of impropriety. His personal honor and integrity were at stake. Could such incidents be coincidental? He began to panic.

He wanted to leave Homoródszentmárton immediately to seek safety. His only hope was his beloved sister Julianna in Székelyudvarhely. She would come and stay with him during the New Year services. Then they would leave together, forever. He called but got no answer. She must have left to visit her children. Imre didn't know what to do.

It is one thing to contemplate suicide, but to be compelled morally to end his disgraced existence was a much more gruesome prospect.

His good parishioner Gyula Szász tried to persuade him to move to their house for a while. They were poor but would take care of him lovingly. "He will find me. There is no escape for me. My life is in danger," Imre cried out. But wasn't his fear less about a madman and more about having been discredited before his congregation? How could the true situation be told and would anyone believe him?

He forced himself to remember that he was a minister first of all, and his duties toward his church came first. He wrote out his resignation:

> Undersigned, Unitarian minister, considering my situation in this congregation, the accusations against me and the failure of my work for fifteen years, I hereby resign from my ministry in Homoródszentmárton effective January 15, 1980. I ask His Eminency the Bishop to take the necessary measures.

> Homoródszentmárton, December 31, 1979
> Imre Gellérd, Minister

Imre handed his resignation to the church's lay president István Timár, who glanced at it with little realization of the weight of his minister's act, and casually stuffed it into his pocket. He mumbled something about the attacker being teased by his fellow drunks in the pub, which explained his rage, and that's all.... Then he left the minister alone.

Nobody came to see Imre in the afternoon. Ordinarily on such a holiday his parishioners would fill his room, enjoying a glass of brandy and wishing each other Happy New Year. He needed someone's closeness, a word of comfort to fend off the impenetrable darkness. A gesture of compassion would have saved him, but his people were lying low, perhaps in indifference, perhaps in guilt, perhaps in fear. Imre's instinct to seek help was still strong. He called his Bishop several times, but nobody answered. His son had left to spend New Year's Eve at a resort. How much now Imre regretted canceling his son's New Year's party.

New Year's Eve worship service usually attracted a large crowd of parishioners. They would take farewell from the old year and greet the new in prayers and singing. Imre was barely able to walk to the church. He had difficulty speaking and choked saying the prayer. He had never been so emotional in church before, not even after prison. After church service the minister normally shook hands with each of his parishioners and extended good wishes, but this time he could not face them. He climbed up to the organ loft and proceeded to sing and play traditional Christmas carols on the organ—as his final farewell. He tape-recorded them for his children. He could see through the window that his congregation was listening from the courtyard, yet no one waited long enough to invite him to join in celebration. This was his loneliest night, when it seemed that even God abandoned him.

The Escape

The church was unusually full for New Year's Day worship service. Rev. Gellérd put on his ministerial robe but did not climb to the pulpit. Speaking from the Lord's Table, he told his congregation that he no longer could serve as their minister. After the attempts of character defamation against him, he said, he could not stand in that pulpit any more. He did not carelessly use the plural. There were other defaming rumors besides the drunken man's accusation. Although they were unfounded, and the gossipers probably did not mean their malice, in his present state of mind it no longer mattered. The village's silence affirmed a sense of complicity. It was their silence that spoke now.

Skipping lunch he left for Lókod, his beloved little church, where he would always find healing. Walking through the snowfield alone, he drew comfort at seeing that Zizi's footsteps along with his own were still recognizable from Christmas Day. The footprints would soon fade, just as his life would. How he longed for his children at these moments. At Lókod he preached a conclusion of his ministry, from the pulpit this time, but forgot to tape-record it. By the time he finished supper in the welcoming home of the lay president, it was already dark. Ordinarily, he walked home the five kilometers, but this time, this only time, he asked his host to take him by his horse-drawn sleigh. He would like to say good-bye to the Homoród valley, he told him. He added, "In case I never come back, please give my last salary to my children." He did not intend to dramatize his farewell, but these S.O.S. signals just slipped out of his mouth. No one heard it, no one! Nobody asked him what his trouble was, or whether he was all right. Were the souls of those people more callused than their hands?

He had stepped onto the slope and he did not know how to stop the avalanche he had set forth.

He went home alone to his cold grave. He swallowed the entire bottle of *Teperin,* a strong antidepressant pill he had requested from Zizi for his cousin.

He had already recorded his farewell to his children the night before.

"I must not think of them now lest I die of heartbreak," he thought. Soon a strange euphoria freed him from his unbearable anxiety as he realized, triumphantly, how he would fool the Securitate when they came to arrest him. They turned his village against him, or just into silent lambs. He was no longer strong enough to withstand the torture. He could have been coerced to become an informer and harm others, and he would rather die than destroy somebody. He would slip out of their grip—forever! He would be free at last. Free as never before! Strangely, he was almost grateful for the madman's assault. Without that final push, he would still be around, hesitating. His ambivalence would not have let him go like this.

The state of fading away brought up memories of his agony at the prison camp and everything seemed familiar. With his whole being, he held onto his consciousness. While his life was escaping him, he tried to hold onto its meaning. He was hovering over the abyss, calling unto the deep, the depth of the One. *Abyssum invocat abyssum.* And yet, he still hoped for being rescued. He would bring back this eternal freedom with him. *Then* he would be redeemed forever.

CHAPTER 12

Over the Abyss

H overing...brings the rapture of liberation. Light so bright it engulfs me, bliss so intense it turns me irresistibly toward it. Secrets of life and death decoding...I can see, I can hear beyond the boundaries of my senses.

I hear my son crying! I cannot leave him. I must give him a chance.... He was dancing when I reached for him. He sensed it but did not understand what was happening to him, why he began to weep uncontrollably. His friends were bewildered when he decided to leave the party and head home to his mother.

Soon he will be at the side of my bed. I can die in peace when I am assured of his love. I can give my final blessing.

Death was simple, I had thought. Trapped and having no way out, I wanted to return to my Creator. I am fleeing life in a cowardly manner, I know, and I still want to return. I cried for help everywhere, but no one understood, as if a transparent wall separated me from people around.

A mere spectator now, I am fascinated about the chances I still have for life; chances for those who try to rescue me with repentant zeal. I would like to yell, "It is too late!" The chances are canceling out each other.

My good parishioner came this morning to see how I made it through the night. Because he found my front door still locked at ten o'clock, he assumed that I must have left for the city. He even sealed his assumption by locking my outside gate and hanging my key on the conventional place, which meant, "The minister is not home, don't even look." I had an urge to shake him." "Look, search, someone is in danger! Listen to your intuition!" A few people came by during the morning to see me, but they had no chance—the gate locked, the key outside, I was gone! I soon will be, but there is still time, still some time on my side.

Had Zizi's lover arrived, now he too would have been fooled. Through him I had the only real chance for being rescued. I was waiting for him. I left my woodcarving on the table for his son, but they did not make it to my birthday. It had been snowing heavily *all night long. He and his son left in the morning to arrive at my house by lunch. They got stuck in the huge snow at the top of the very first mountain pass, so they barely got back to Marosv·s·rhely. Once home, he called me by phone. "He must have left home, he doesn't answer," the postal and phone clerk concluded. But the composer impatiently yelled, "It is impossible, he is expecting our visit. He must be home. Please, go immediately and check on him!" The annoyed clerk flatly refused to obey this order. It was not her job to check on people. She won this one, and my rescuer tried to cope with his irrational behavior. "Am I the Dalai Lama after all, to act upon a mere premonition?" He reluctantly gave up trying to contact me.*

Circumstances seemed to conglomerate in an unlikely scenario, as if purposefully preventing me from escaping death. Death must have learned the game that my life has always played with me, teasingly presenting the desired goal and giving me the ability to reach it, then shattering it at the very last moment. Now that I can clearly see the pattern of life and death intertwined, I worry about such consistency.

I choose life, although now it will be eternal life.

My good parishioner's worries remained unsettled and he came back to the parsonage at 2 p.m. It was only then that he discovered the light on in my room. Alarmed, he broke into my house. I was so sorry for his remorse. He called the doctor, who called the ambulance. While they lifted me to dress me in warm clothes, I stopped breathing. Not to scare them, but I just did not need to breathe. I was light like a butterfly. The good doctor, however, heroically resuscitated me. I collaborated with him, for I knew from Zizi how glorious it is for a doctor to bring a patient back to life. She has just done it, and that is her birthday gift to me.

* * *

Hopelessness took over people in the parsonage as they waited for the ambulance in vain. It actually had left the city hospital promptly, but the seventeen kilometers took it more than an hour on the snowed-in road. Then something went fatally wrong. The ambulance went to the wrong village and returned to the hospital without the patient. Two hours, three more hours passed.... It was sunset by the time the ambulance took Imre to the hospital.

Andor had just arrived there! He was unable to comprehend the inevitable. This was not supposed to happen after he finally found his father and his father found him. The new relationship was more meaningful than anything before. Why would God take away his gift? If he had just insisted on spending the New Year with his father! "Wake up Dad, I am begging you, don't leave me again!"

His father was in a deep coma, his breathing heavy, loud, with long periods of apnea. The doctor on duty underplayed the situation. There was no respirator in the hospital, and the heavy snow was reason enough not to send him to a larger hospital. The patient was a hopeless case anyway. Life was cheap in Eastern Europe.

But I am the father of two children!

Thunder

Events during hospital duty in Budapest were never unexpected, but the appearance of Zizi's mother-in-law was. She was rushed to the hospital where Zizi was on duty. While Zizi was examining her, she went into a cardiac arrest. Without a properly equipped emergency room and with the help of just a single nurse, Zizi successfully resuscitated her. This was the first resuscitation in her medical career and she was ecstatic. Saving a life would be her birthday gift to her father, Zizi decided. "Guess what my surprise is to you, Dad?" she was rehearsing while trying to make a phone connection again to her father's village. She could almost his ecstatic voice, "Oh, Zizi!" She had to wait for the phone connection for a couple of hours. The wait was a sweet anticipation, imagining sitting at her father's dinner table with his guests. She wondered how traumatic turning sixty might be for him.

The phone connection was finally established. "Happy birthday to you, happy birthday to you...," she sang into the receiver.

It was not her father who responded but the clerk from the village post office. "I'm afraid I have terrible news for you. Your father was found unconscious in his home. The ambulance has just taken him to the hospital." Through an instant connection switch, now her mother was at the other end of the line. "Your father is in a deep coma. Nobody knows what happened. While the physician was examining him, he had a cardiac arrest and was in a state of clinical death, but he was resuscitated. The doctors in the hospital are speculating that the cause was poisoning. The villagers talked about a physical assault against him." "Get the best specialist, my former professor from the clinics! You must save him! Do the impossible! He must live, he must!" yelled Zizi. The connection was suddenly cut off. God had never been beseeched the way Zizi did; her prayer was frantic.

You can turn this nightmare around, you can save my father's life, don't take him away from us, not yet, his life is not finished, he has never been happy yet, still waiting for your blessings, life owes him, you, God, owe him, he is your servant, pastor of your flock, God have mercy on him, have mercy on us, do a miracle if that is what it takes, you can, you must, he is still alive, keep him alive, I must see him, I must, we have to have time together, we never had time, time, we need more time, together, you owe him time, you owe him happiness, he has so much to give, he has been building your Kingdom, God, you have invested so much in him, let his talents bear fruit, let him be a father to his son a little longer, he needs his father, he has just found him, his heart will break, his life will break without his father, we cannot live with that much guilt, let us repent, we need time, our father needs time, our church needs him, he is only fifty-nine, give those prison years back to him now, he needs time! He needs love, but we need time to show him our love, he must know love, more love, love him God, let him live, he is still alive and you have the almighty power over his life or death, choose life for him, you can do it, it is still not too late. I implore you, I will serve you with my entire life, with my whole being, in any way you wish me to, just give my father back, God!

God, hear me!

Zizi fell asleep before dawn, and a vivid dream captured her. In it her father appeared in her hospital at the top of the staircase. He blissfully said to her, "Here I am, I came to you!" She wanted to rush to him, to fly into his arms, but the telephone woke her up. It was the dreaded, dreaded call.

"Your father has died a few minutes ago." Her mother's voice was the messenger of death.

"No!!" Zizi lost her mind. Heaven and earth collapsed around her. The universe reverberated in her immeasurable loss. For those last hours the boundary of life and death seemed fluid. God had the choice and the power. Her father had a chance. Hers was hope. While saving a life, she lost her father's.

Life suddenly lost its meaning for her; it was death, lusty, hungry death, a total darkness.

It was January the 3rd, 1980, her father's sixtieth birthday.

Bound by Light

My eyes have seen thy glory and my son, let me come to you, Lord.

I don't deserve your grace, for I have broken my son's heart. He is sitting at my bedside, he is holding my hands and this is bliss in itself. How much I would like to tell him about the glory of the Light, the freedom without boundaries! He sees only darkness in death.

I have now a glimpse into eternal healing...the lure of Light, God's embrace so irresistible....

Falling, forever, with no return! Help me! I want to live!

I want to tell my children...I am losing my...There is no air...I am suffocating. I must breathe, I must! I must write this down for them....

Zizi, Andorka, my dear angels, my precious children, good-bye....

My hand is failing, my thoughts are failing...it is finished. Lord, save me, save me...this is dying...being no more....

At the dawn of my sixtieth birthday, the doctor is suddenly talking about me in the past tense. With this I am free to visit Zizi in her hospital. Her hopes for my rescue were tenacious. She must now find comfort in my last words that I wrote in my notebook: "Live life divinely."

* * *

The always caressing hands were lifeless. His searching, fiery eyes gazed openly into eternity. The last words, Andorka, Zizi, were frozen on those lips. The veil of death slowly crawled between them. Andor desperately tried to hold him back from stepping onto the starry path. There was no greater loss than his.

His father's clothes were hanging abandoned on the hospital rack the next morning—a mold of a life, a sacred shroud.

EPILOGUE

Death occurred without a clinical diagnosis. Rumors about a possible assault made forensic autopsy unavoidable. No one should ever see one's parent on the autopsy table as Andor did. The day of his funeral, January 5, 1980, in the Unitarian cemetery of Székelyudvarhely, was the coldest day on record. An immense snow buried the houses and the roads of Transylvania. The world was peaceful, like death. Imre wore his ministerial robe and all the suffering of the world on his face. The open casket laid in state in the First Unitarian Church of Székelyudvarhely, his childhood church, instead of his last parish Homoródszentmárton. One would not have expected many people to come to the funeral in such weather, but when church bells tolled for Imre Gellérd, a huge crowd gathered. Seventy Unitarian ministers braved the cold, coming from the farthest villages. Robed in the traditional ministerial black capes, they took turns standing as the guard of honor around the casket.

Representatives from the Unitarian Headquarters were notably absent from the funeral. Perhaps it was considered a dangerous political statement to participate in Imre Gellérd's funeral. The Bishop, who traditionally buried ministers, was down with the flu. Only Imre's faithful friend and prisonmate Rev. László Székely came from Kolozsvár.

Rev. Dénes Szász, Dean of Imre's district and minister of the First Unitarian Church of Székelyudvarhely, announced from the pulpit that the authority for him to perform the funeral came from the deceased. A few weeks earlier Imre bluntly and for no apparent reason, had said to his colleague, "Remember, you have the duty to bury me." The Dean had tried to overcome his surprise with a ministerial joke. Like Imre's other cries for help, this too was ignored. Then it was taken as the authority for claiming the honor of preaching the funeral sermon.

In his sermon Rev. Szász speculated about the cause of death. Suffering from chronic insomnia, Imre had used sedatives, and one night he had crossed the threshold and slipped into death by accident. "There was no match for Imre Gellérd's outstanding qualities in our church's recent history," he eulogized.

God blessed him with such intense light of the intellect and of the spirit, which shined way beyond his space and time. His personality had a charisma that attracted those who were seeking God. He was our burning bush of Mount Horeb. His flames reached the skies and threw their light into the future. Not even death will extinguish his light. Why couldn't he rise higher? Because of an unjust world and because of his own personality traits. He had extraordinary talent but no ability for positioning himself in the political arena of the church in order to survive.

The next speaker Rev. László Székely continued,

The gap between his high soaring and his awareness of reality was too wide. His genius and humility did not join with practicality and a common sense for diplomacy. He had extreme emotional surges from lethargy to ecstasy. He conquered the tallest of mountains but fell on small pebbles. His inner struggle was as strong as his light. Perhaps because he burned so intensely, he burned himself out so early. When he was bleeding internally, no word of comfort reached him, no hand caressed him in compassion. He was alone. The torch, while illuminating the path for others, consumed itself. His was an essential loneliness from which he could not free himself, and which consumed his soul. His beloved poet, Endre Ady, expressed this best:

> I am no heir, no proud ancestor,
> I have no friend, nor brother and sister,
> I have never belonged,
> I have never belonged.

> I am, like every human, highness,
> Iceberg, enigma, strange and timeless,
> Distant Will-o'-the-wisp,
> Distant Will-o'-the-wisp.

> But, oh, I can't remain unspoken,
> I have to bare myself wide open,
> Behold me, everyone,
> Behold me, everyone.

In all self-torture, in every song,
I want to be loved, to belong.
Belong to somebody,
Belong to somebody.[1]

The funeral procession of black mourners was a kilometer long. The crisp snow under thousands of boots was the only funeral music. The open grave was like a fresh wound in the immense whiteness. The burial ritual continued at the graveside in minus 30 degrees Celsius. Jeremiah Lamentations 5:16, "The crown is fallen from our head!" was the text of Rev. Dénes Benczö's farewell speech in the name of Transylvania's Unitarian ministers. A year before while repairing the steeple of Homródszentmárton, Rev. Gellérd was holding the other end of the rope to secure him. Now Rev. Benczö held the rope to lower his friend's casket into the frozen earth. He preached with great power:

The well has dried up, the tree has withered, the light gone out. You nourished the spiritually thirsty. The tree of your immense knowledge and wide horizon gave us security, hope, and peace. You elevated us. You rekindled our vision when ordinary life and smallness blinded us. You were the way toward the peaks, toward the realm of higher pursuits. The crown is fallen from our head! He who saved us in our desperation had nobody to save him.

The great burden of your life was that you had the ability to see farther, soar higher, create more abundantly than any of us had. And we are afraid of those who have more talent, have wider vision and knowledge, those who are more accomplished human beings than the rest of us. You kept proclaiming—preaching, singing, roaring—your dreams that elucidated the way for us to make our church and our world more human. We never had the courage to recognize that we were dressing our impoverished spirit with your light, the beauty of your intellect and soul. You so freely shared them with us. As a master of practical theology, you have created more values in it than most of your famous predecessors did. Who will nurture our spirit and intellect from now on? Your light now is our light. May your seeds that you have sown so

[1] "I Want to Be Loved" by Endre Ady, translated by Peter Zollman, *Quest of the Miracle Stag*, Edited by Adam Makkay.

abundantly bring forth harvest in the next generation. We will always stay in the shadow of your light and indebted to you forever.

He let the rope down and the earth pounded on the casket.

* * *

They think my death was an accident! That I was depressed, paranoid, that I slipped into death by mistake. I left them multiple messages, but they haven't found them yet. They don't know that I was pushed over the edge by political pressure and a multi-pronged conspiracy. They could not see the manipulations of the system. They don't know that I would have been arrested soon. How blind, how deaf they are.

Even my death, my chosen death, my ultimate, desperate protest went wrong! My protest against dehumanization, against a lifetime of intimidation by the Securitate and its instruments is interpreted as a stupid drug overdose! How disgraceful!

It was not my desire to become a martyr, a witness to injustice and inhumanity. To carry my destiny all the way until the ultimate indictment of an evil regime, but to give my life in protest—that was my choice. But now the very dignity of my suffering and death is taken away from me. My last right to protest is trivialized.

I have given up life, and I must give up on the blissful union with my Creator. I must resist the Light that lures me. I must stay involved with my life's aftermath. I am trapped, once again, in the waiting. Will they realize the truth? Only truth liberates me, finally, from my prison walls.

* * *

After the funeral the church consistory of Homoródszentmárton and the family met to unseal the parsonage—and face the vale of tears. Imre's church treasury was a cardboard box in his wardrobe. Everybody knew this place. While they counted the money, Imre's friend made a discrete sign toward Zizi and Andor to follow him to the side room. He discovered something alarming on the cover of the box. It was Imre's handwriting, not his pearly letters but a barely legible scrawl. It took some time to realize its nature, and for its meaning to unfold. It was Imre's hastily improvised last will. The handwriting preserved the state of his fading consciousness before entering the realm of no return. These were his last instructions:

> *Pay the church bell-ringer his salary.*
> *My books shall belong to Andorka.*
> *Sell the plum brandy.*
> *My grave shall be in the Homoródszentmárton cemetery.*
> *Give some of my clothes to my brothers, but Julianna should receive the most.*
> *My theological works shall go to Tomika and Sanyika [young ministers].*
> *Collect the backpayment from members of the Homoródszentmárton church.*
> *Don't allow the Church to make my grave mark. You, yourselves take care of it.*
> *Bury me with music.*
> *Give my ministerial robe to a good seminary student.*
> *I am the one to be blamed for everything, I must atone.*
> *I have been loved, but Julianna was an angel to me.*
> *The 1,000 lei for calendars, mail it to the Bishop's office, also on behalf of Lókod.*
> *Pay the taxes.*
> *It will be so good to sleep.*
> *I loved my parishioners, I loved them very much!*
> *My farewell is on the tape recorder.*
> *The secret police will arrest me soon. I cannot undergo that doom any more.*

The last sentence was illegible to the family for many years. Imre's disciple Rev. Dénes Farkas finally solved the puzzle, the key to the mystery.

Only then, through this horrifying revelation, did they suddenly realize that their father had committed suicide.

"Do you realize how misfortune haunted our Dad even into his death?" Zizi said to her brother.

"We have failed him even in fulfilling his last wishes. We buried him in the wrong place. He instructed us carefully, though. Could he have imagined that no one would have looked at the moneybox before the funeral?"

To touch the tape recording where their father's greatest secret lay felt like a brutish intrusion into the mystery of being in between life and death. His spirit, anguished by the ultimate dilemma, *to be or not to be*, was now captured for eternity:

My dearest Zizi and Andorka! Please forgive me and don't condemn me for my act, which I had to carry out. My life, unfortunately, has no meaning any more. I was a target of repeated abuses and insults. I consider my life in danger. Not just for what happened at Ilona's house. I was informed that I, we, will be soon arrested. Therefore, it will be better for me in this way. Please, forgive me! I cannot ask you to forget me, that must not happen. May God bless you! Care for each other, love each other. Be good persons. May God bless both of you to rise to ever greater peaks in life and to be happy. I had a very sad New Year's Eve. But it is finished now.... I beg for your forgiveness. Good-bye! With your names on my lips, my life will end, everything will be over. My dear Angels, my precious children, good-bye.

His voice choked with sobbing.